THE MEDIUM

Papa
Mirek
& Kathi ♡

THE MEDIUM EXPLOSION

A Guide to Navigating the World of Those Who Claim to Communicate with the Dead

ROBERT GINSBERG

Waterside Productions

Printed in the United States of America

First Printing, 2021

ISBN-13: 978-1-951805-48-7 print edition
ISBN-13: 978-1-951805-49-4 ebook edition

Waterside Productions

2055 Oxford Ave
Cardiff, CA 92007
www.waterside.com

DEDICATION

To my wife of forty-six years, Phran Rosenbaum Ginsberg, who has now passed into spirit. She was my guide, mentor, and life partner, and not having her in the physical world is heartbreaking. In her final days she was asked her opinion on the meaning of life. She replied, "it's simple… to leave this world a better place." That she certainly did, literally touching the lives of thousands in a positive way.

ACKNOWLEDGEMENTS

This book would not have been possible without the guidance, wisdom, and support of my wife Phran, who now continues her work from the realm of spirit. Her intellect, passion and logical mind never cease to amaze me. I am grateful for all of the Certified Mediums and scientists with whom I have worked over the years, and special thanks go to the following mediums who have contributed accounts published in this book: Janet Mayer (janetmayer.net), Doreen Molloy (doreenmolloy.com), Angelina Diana (angelinadiana.com), Laura Lynne Jackson (lauralynnejackson.com), Lynn LeClere (lynnthemedium.com), Janet Nohavec (janetnohavec.com), Rebecca LoCicero (rebeccaannelocicero.com), and Joseph Shiel (josephpshiel.com). Special thanks to afterlife historian Michael Tymn (http://whitecrowbooks.com/michaeltymn), scholars Piero Calvi-Parisetti. MD (drparisetti.com), Betty Kovacs, PhD (kamlak.com), and researcher Dianne Arcangel MS for their solid work in the field. I am grateful to all the dedicated volunteers of Forever Family Foundation for their selfless work towards the greater good and helping the bereaved.

CONTENTS

INTRODUCTION

On a summer day in 2001 I remember playing golf with a friend of mine who recently lost his wife to cancer. While sitting in a golf cart with him waiting to tee off at the next hole, he turned to me in a somewhat subdued manner and confessed that he had just visited a medium. Immediately alarm bells started resonating in my brain as I thought, "Uh-oh, my friend Kenny has snapped." He went on to tell me that the medium communicated very specific pieces of information from his deceased wife that the medium could not have known, and he was now convinced that his wife survived physical death. While telling me of his experience he must have picked up on the glazed look in my eyes, and said "You don't believe any of this, do you?" As much as I wanted to support my friend, all I could manage to mutter was something like "not really, but who knows." I remember returning home that day and telling my wife that I was worried about my friend Kenny, as he was being taken advantage of by a huckster.

Shortly after this encounter with my friend in 2001 my life took an abrupt change, a change that I never could have imagined. Circumstances catapulted me into the world of mediums, those who purport having the ability to communicate with the dead. After almost twenty years of investigation and exploration in this area I have reached my own conclusions about the way mediums work and their abilities. This book is a guide to help you navigate the murky waters of mediumship and will hopefully answer many of the questions you may have about communication with those who are no longer embodied.

THE OVERVIEW

Chances are that if you noticed the title and are reading this book you are aware of the proliferation of psychics, mediums, and spiritual advisors that set up shop in virtually every neighborhood, all claiming the ability to talk to the dead. You certainly have noticed their on-line presence and have most likely taken note of the many media projects that incorporate topics that defy mainstream thinking. Some would view this ever-growing population of practitioners as a blight set upon our communities and an insult to our intelligence. I fit into this school of thought for much of my adult life, as I thought believing in life after death was akin to believing in Santa Claus, a nice fairy tale but one that should not be entertained by those with a modicum of intelligence. Others will insist that these seers of the future and portals to a world beyond are indeed real and fulfill an important role. Truth be told, the great majority in this metaphysical group are fraudulent, delusional, or woefully underdeveloped. However, there are some that can absolutely do what they claim, and there is substantial empirical, anecdotal, and experiential evidence that points to life after physical death. This book will touch upon such evidence but its focus is specifically about mediums and the goal is to educate the readers as they wade through the world of "mediumshit" to identify true "mediumship." There may be some terms used throughout the book of which you are unfamiliar, so a glossary is provided at the end.

Mediumship enjoyed great popularity in the late 19th and early 20th centuries, as people regularly gathered in séances in attempts to contact the dead. The doctrine of Spiritism, the belief in the existence of non-physical entities, spread among the masses and contributed to the religious movement of Spiritualism. Spiritualist centers opened by the thousands across the globe, and well-respected researchers started investigating mediums in attempts to not only determine if the phenomenon was real, but to isolate the mechanism that made it possible. People were rejecting the prevailing materialistic view of science as they contemplated the bigger picture. However, interest in mediums among the masses started to wane at the end of 1920s as the cycle turned toward physical science. There were many reasons for the decline, none more important than the fraud that was uncovered as many high-profile mediums were found to be less than honest.

However, I believe that we have never seen the likes of the current explosion of interest and sheer number of practitioners. Some of the reasons for the renewed popularity of those who purport to communicate with the dead appear to be obvious. The media has jumped on the interest full throttle, with a seemingly endless number of television shows involving mediums, psychics, and paranormal investigators. Books about the afterlife, written from both experiential and scientific perspectives, have often topped best-seller lists. Some of the largest grossing movies in recent history have incorporated paranormal and afterlife themes. Mainstream publications have also begun to tackle the associated subjects of non-local consciousness, telepathy, near death experiences, intention and healing, reincarnation, deathbed visions, electronic voice phenomena and other experiences that defy accepted science. Unfortunately, most of the media attention is not the result of a desire to learn the truth, but the motivation is financial gain as they gain audience by sensationalizing the paranormal.

The strong interest in life after death has been with us since the ancients, and the reasons for such contemplation are numerous. I suspect that anyone who claims never to have even thought about the possibility of life after death is not being truthful. Perhaps our interest simply emanates from the fear of our own mortality, as the prospect of being extinguished forever is too much for some to bear. Personally, I spent much of my life dreading the prospect of no longer existing. As far as I was concerned, one's identity was determined by the brain, and the measure of who we are was based upon intellectual firepower and material possessions. However, in the back of my mind it never made any sense for one to simply disappear, and the thought of being extinguished reinforced the feeling of helplessness and randomness. So, despite all the outward trappings of what most would term to be success, a nagging sense of despair would often rise to the forefront. I think that many of the ills that we now face as a society are the direct result of such thinking. Although we often bury the thought in our subconscious, we are all very much aware of the fact that everyone dies. The way in which we deal with this knowledge varies greatly from person to person and directly affects our quality of life. Death anxiety can take control and influence our actions as we navigate our physical lives. On the other hand, knowledge of other realms of existence, along with a sense of connectedness, can provide much peace and allow fuller and more meaningful lives.

I find that some people ask why we should even care if anything happens after death. It may be a philosophical question, but people give many common responses when posed with this question:

- The religious person might answer by stating that there most definitely is life after death, and we better care as such after-death existence will be either heaven-like or hellish depending upon how many rules you abided by or disregarded.
- The spiritual person will often state that we should care about the love and compassion that we show in the physical, as our actions here will influence our existence in the spiritual realm. They will also point out that our transition process includes self – examination and self – judgment, as opposed to an appearance before an all-knowing examiner or panel with a checklist.
- Those on the fence about life after death often express their hope that life continues, but do not spend a great deal of

time in contemplation of the possibility, at least not until they reach old age. They care but are not sure and do not see much value in focusing on things that they cannot control. They sometimes hedge their bet by trying to be the best that they can be, just in case. Others do the opposite and engage in not so nice things, as it is just as likely that death is final and there are no repercussions.

- Pragmatists will cite the lack of any legitimate evidence of survival and will not concern themselves with such fanciful thoughts. Whereas the spiritual people don't fear death because of an inner knowing that life continues, the pragmatist will often state that they also don't fear death because there are no feelings or thoughts after death, only nothingness, so they won't be missing anything or anyone, or even know that they are dead.

- The close-minded skeptics will readily tell you that you should not care simply because such a possibility does not exist. However, I suspect that it is the skeptic who cares the most.

Many believe that there must be some purpose and meaning to our physical lives, as the thought of being a random automaton is simply not acceptable. Of course, if our lives have meaning, belief in life after death becomes logical, as a continuing progression through other realms of existence fits the plan of a continuum of growth and development. It is true that all organized religions stress such meaning, purpose, and various types of afterlife existence, but such beliefs most often come with strings attached. If you do this and this, then you will have such and such. Blind faith is perfectly acceptable and comforting for some, but others prefer to see some evidence.

The reality is that intuitive processes and communication with the deceased preceded organized religion, and some ancient civilizations incorporated contact with the dead as part of daily life. It was just the way it was and certainly not thought of as being paranormal. Grecian civilization included the use of psychomanteums, sensory deprivation chambers where people went to converse with loved ones in spirit. There have been indigenous cultures in history that communicated among themselves telepathically, a normal part of life that came with the knowledge that mind extends beyond brain. Other societies regularly met to discuss their dreams and visions, and then acted accordingly in their planning and activities. Shamans, yogis, and adepts entered (and still do) altered states of consciousness to gain knowledge and insights from elders who reside in the spirit realm. The fact is that our ancestors knew something that we have yet to learn. Mystic traditions dominated civilization for tens of thousands of years, and recent discoveries have shown that the original founders of today's organized religions were products of such ancient wisdom.

But is there a deeper reason why we are presently seeing such a renewed interest in communication with the dead? Yes, the media has played a part, but that is just a reflection of the general interest. Perhaps more of us are seeking explanations as the world in which we live appears to have more conflict, atrocities, hunger, and natural disasters than ever before. A bigger picture could lend some order to the chaos. Or could it be that those in spirit have decided to take a renewed interest in helping us to recognize what truly matters? If that were the case, perhaps there are more mediums today because there are more of the deceased that want to communicate to those in the physical realm. This might be part of the new paradigm of consciousness that is often discussed among people who believe that we are more than our physical bodies.

Huge numbers of people regularly have afterlife encounters. Sometimes these communications are summarily dismissed as such experiences do not fall within the boundaries taught to us by science, religion, culture, and logic. But they still occur. The change upon which we are now embarking is that larger numbers of people are willing to talk about such things publicly. When people are put in an environment where they feel that they will not be judged, the floodgates open as they relate astounding experiences that were kept inside for years or decades.

When we talk about life after death, commonly referred to as survival of consciousness, what is it that survives? Surely it is not our physical bodies, as they truly are no more. What continues is our mind (consciousness or soul if you prefer), and along with it our personalities and certain memories. Most have a hard time imagining existence as an entity of only thought and energy, as we spend our physical lives defining who we are as our bodies. However, there is an overwhelming amount of evidence that our minds can indeed act independently of our physical brains, and consciousness is not confined to the area inside our skulls. If one chooses to accept the evidence of mind to mind communication, commonly termed "non-local," then the concept of our true selves continuing after physical death becomes much more palatable, if not logical.

So, what about all this stuff you have been hearing about – is it real? Can people communicate mind to mind, despite being separated by great distances? Do near death experiencers really visit the afterlife before returning to the physical world? Do people close to death have visions in which they see their loved ones who have passed before them? Are mediums really talking to the dead? Can people in the spirit world imprint their voices on recording devices? Do some of us return to the physical world after spending some time in the spirit world? Is after-death communication possible and can discarnates (the dead) communicate with the physical realm in various ways?

When you look at the established scientific evidence collected over the years, and consider the body of research in its entirety, it sure appears that the only plausible answer is "Yes!" Science has not been able to isolate the mechanism that allows such phenomena but has been able to verify that they exist. Some in mainstream research choose to ignore the evidence, but the evidence exists, nonetheless.

However, the purpose of this book is not to discuss the various types of evidence and the published research in depth. It is meant to provide practical information about the process of mediumship only. Mediums have been studied by some of the finest scientific minds for more than 150 years, most concluding that some people can communicate with the dead. The key word here is some people. There are tens of thousands of psychic and medium practitioners in the United States and around the globe who cannot do what they claim. Some are out and out frauds, some are well-meaning but underdeveloped, and others are gifted but still incorporate unethical practices in their readings. We must question whether this explosion of mediums is something to be feared or controlled, and if we are facing a scourge of practitioners ready and willing to give false hope for profit. Or, as mentioned previously, is the sudden influx of new mediums simply the result of a shift in consciousness, with people beginning to recognize that they are more than their physical bodies? Perhaps, as I suspect, it is a combination of both.

Qualified mediums can fulfill an important role and help others to lead more meaningful lives. However, the prospect of a fraud sitting with the bereaved makes my skin crawl. Taking advantage of the most fragile among us is despicable and reflective of a society that often seeks out prey for their own materialistic gain. Those who desperately want to connect with deceased loved ones are among the most vulnerable to misinformation and deceit, and there are no regulatory bodies that offer true protection from the frauds. People in grief will very often pay any amount and go anywhere for even the slightest prospect of communicating with their deceased loved one. I am saddened to see a booming cottage industry of practitioners that are often poison to the bereaved and detrimental to the legitimate people in the field. We are now seeing a full throttle explosion of "wannamediums," a category that includes wanting to become a medium for a variety of different reasons. I will go so far as to call it an epidemic, with all the negative implications suggested by the term. This group includes those who want to become mediums simply for monetary gain, those who want to feel self-important and delude themselves into believing that they are helping others, outright hucksters and frauds, and well-meaning aspirants who may have some intuitive ability but cannot connect with discarnate entities.

Some might argue that we should not be so concerned with fraudulent mediums. They view the entire community as fraudulent, so there is no such thing as a medium that is not a fraud. That is why it is so important to have a means of discerning the good mediums from the bad. It is unlike any other profession or trade. There are fraudulent medical practitioners, financial advisors, attorneys, etc., but few would make the claim that all within each category are deceitful. All these other professions have regulatory bodies that institute mandatory ethical compliance and set standards for proficiency. This is not so in the mediumship world, and the scientists and practitioners who work in this realm must be more diligent than their colleagues who are engaged in other pursuits.

This book will show you how to navigate through the medium world, a world that is often fraught with disappointment, but can also result in a life changing experience. We will give you practical information that you can use, including the various types of mediumship, the differences between psychics and mediums, cold reading techniques, what constitutes real evidence and warning signs to observe, how you can score your own readings, and the do's and don'ts when sitting with a medium. Personal and true accounts are included in this book to provide insight into what constitutes significant after death communication. However, to protect privacy, some of the names have been changed.

Much of the information presented in this guide has come out of prior research, personal experiences, and my own observations from the Medium Certification Evaluation Process of Forever Family Foundation. I'll need to start with some basic background, as I must disclose that I am not a scientist, simply a well – informed person who was pointed in this direction as a bereaved parent, and give you some insight into how I approached the subject of life after death.

If you would have asked me eighteen years ago what I thought of mediums, I probably would have replied that they were a bunch of fraudulent roving fortune tellers. Firmly entrenched in materialist thinking, pure logic told me that there was no possible way for our consciousness to survive our physical deaths. What could survive? Our bodies quickly decompose after death, our brains are who we are, so therefore the notion that we continue to live on is ridiculous and fanciful thinking

In the early morning hours of September 1, 2002, my wife Phran awakened and sat up in bed looking ashen and deeply troubled. When I asked what was wrong, she said "something horrible is going to happen today." No details, just the overwhelming knowledge of impending doom. How seriously would you take such a dire prediction? Even though I did not believe in any of this "stuff" I decided to take it as seriously as she did. The evidence forced me to do so, as there were other times in our lives together when Phran had precognitive experiences that later turned out to be true. They were all good things, but if she had been right then it was logical to assume that she could be right now.

When faced with the possibility of grave trouble, every parent thinks of their children, and we checked on our three children throughout the day. My oldest was working one last day in his summer job before returning to college the next day at the University of Delaware. My middle child was already at Carnegie Mellon University, eagerly embarking upon her new college career. I dropped my youngest child Bailey off at her part-time job in town, her last day before returning to high school, a place she loved and adored. We constantly followed the whereabouts of all three throughout the day…just to be sure. By the time evening rolled upon us, I relaxed more and let Phran's premonition fade from my awareness. Phran and I had dinner with my son Jonathan and daughter Bailey in town at one of our favorite haunts. During dinner, Bailey told Phran that she was curious about and studying palmistry and was somewhat distressed. She then showed Phran her hand and related the fact that she determined that she had a "very short lifeline."

On the way home from dinner, Jonathan & Bailey left for home in one car to get started on the school preparations for the next day. Phran and I took our other car and stopped to pick up some essentials, and then also headed for home. On the way home we came upon a horrific accident, and our worst fears were realized. Bailey died at the hospital a few hours later, and Jon was air-lifted to another hospital with brain injuries.

Several months later, when we came to realize that Jonathan would recover and I started to emerge from the shock and entered the abyss of utter despair and sadness, I suddenly remembered the beginning event of that fateful day. I became consumed with finding out how Phran knew about the impending doom. In my mind there were only two possible logical explanations. Either some of us possess the ability to catch a glimpse of the future, or, as hard as it was to entertain, someone was sending Phran a telepathic warning. Of course, if it were the latter, it would raise other issues and questions – did the warning come from the living or from the dead? Could this have been prevented if Phran was better able to interpret the message? I was also devastated by the thought that I could have changed the outcome of this tragedy by making a myriad of different decisions. Why did I allow the kids to drive home after the pre-warning? Why did I not tell them to take the large sedan vs. the sports car that my son rarely drove? There were a hundred other decisions that I could have made that would have changed the outcome, including getting up from our seats at the restaurant ten seconds earlier or later. The guilt was all-consuming, I could not imagine surviving my grief, and I needed to find some answers.

I embarked upon science exploration to find my answers, as I needed to know if it was possible that my daughter still existed in some form. I read about every scientist who conducted research on the possibility that our minds can act independently of our brains, and the survival of consciousness after physical death. I engaged some of these scientists, took part in research, and learned everything I possibly could. I read voraciously, devouring anything and everything on which I could get in my hands. At the same time, Phran needed no such answers from science. She had an inner knowing, something that comes from within and has nothing to do with research.

In the year following Bailey's passing we experienced about twenty occurrences and communications that defied logic and explanation. Phran assured me that these were after death communications. I, on the other hand, dismissed each one as coincidence, and fought the survival hypothesis as hard as I could. Fortunately, I heeded Phran's advice and journaled these experiences as they happened. I went so far as to seek help in calculating the odds against chance of each one happening. After twenty separate occurrences, each with odds against chance exceeding a million to one, even a left brained dunce like me had to relent and change my perspective! The last part of this book will relate some of these personal experiences that changed my way of thinking. I am convinced that first becoming familiar with the scientific research paved the way for my acceptance of these experiences. As you will see, each experience is supported by the scientific research. My willingness to discuss personal experiences is to help illustrate how different my life is now from when I started in my grief. I began in a state of horror, never imagining any respite from my anguish until I died. If I could not wish myself dead, all I wanted to do was crawl into a hole and make the world go away. I was brought up in a world where I believed anything to be possible, and there was always hope of a solution. I now faced something that was impossible to change, a prospect that I could not accept. I desperately wanted to strike a deal with the unseen world, or God, or any entity that could change the course of events. Give me five more minutes with my daughter so that I could give her a hug and tell her how much I loved her, and I would gladly pay with everything I owned, including my own life.

I eventually progressed to the point where I could live my life with meaning and compassion. It was the hardest journey that I ever embarked upon, but one in which I discovered that love and compassion are truly the only pathways to contentment and meaning. As I write these words, I am very much aware of the way I would have reacted to such a statement before my daughter's passing, which would have been with an attitude of disbelief or mockery. I submit that the pathway I took is accessible to all who grieve the loss of a loved one.

As I was putting the finishing touches to this book Phran, my wife of forty-six years, passed into the next world. We were joined at the hip in this physical life, and I have once again been catapulted into a surreal world without her. My grief is profound and pervasive; however, I believe that I will once again survive tragedy due to my knowledge that she still exists in another form and I will see her again.

When it comes to a belief in the afterlife, having a personal experience most often propels one into the *knowing* category. But let us face it, not everyone is fortunate enough to have such an experience. That is why it is so important for us to learn about the different types of evidence that support the premise of other realms of existence. Such knowledge does not always result in one's absolute belief, but it certainly opens the door. I know that in my personal case I dismissed all experiences because I had no frame of reference that would support the concept. I was 100% sure that I never experienced any type of after death communication. But how would I know?

From 2002 to 2004, at the urging of Phran, I visited several mediums even though I did not really believe that any could communicate with the dead. I left the first medium scratching my head and trying to assimilate what had just occurred. Three pieces of information were communicated through the medium from my deceased daughter. Each was extremely specific and something that no person other than my wife could have possibly known. I tried to step back and look at it objectively and wondered if I was making something fit due to my tremendous grief. However, the more I reviewed the experience, the more perplexed I became. I knew that it had to be my daughter mentioning these obscure things, but my logic kept telling me that it was impossible. However, this medium reading opened the door to my search for more evidence, a door I jumped through with great energy and passion. During my search in the year after my daughter's death my wife and I visited a couple of other recommended mediums and were totally unconvinced and disappointed. It was then that we realized the need for a science-based evaluation process for determining the accuracy of individual mediums.

In 2004 Forever Family Foundation (www.foreverfamilyfoundation.org) was birthed, which is an all – volunteer 501c3 not for profit organization that seeks to blur the lines between science and spirituality. Our mission is to educate the public about scientific evidence that suggests we are much more than our physical bodies, further research, and offer support to the bereaved. Many different types of phenomena and disciplines of research fall within our interests, including mediumship. Taking input from several credentialed scientists in the field, we developed a process of evaluating the evidence that mediums communicate. The purpose of the Medium Certification Evaluation Process is simply to provide a reliable resource for the bereaved. The program is conducted free of charge, no medium can pay to be listed on our site, and roughly 90% of the mediums who go through the evaluation fail to receive certification. The core services of Forever Family Foundation including membership are free of charge.

I should also add that I feel it important for us all to remain open-minded skeptics. This is especially important to the bereaved, as one should not blindly accept all phenomena as evidence of a world beyond. If one can identify the true evidence and discount the occurrences that have physical explanations, it will make the reality of survival that much stronger.

BELIEF IN AN AFTERLIFE & THE NATURE OF GRIEF

Death and grief can be thought of as cause and effect, inexorably intertwined, a necessary part of our physical existence. The death part is quite easy to understand, as our physical bodies have a shelf life that can be measured in finite years. Physical death has occurred since the dawn of man, with no exceptions, and with no prospect of this ever changing.

Grief, on the other hand, is an emotion that has always varied in intensity and can take many forms. When we speak of grief as it relates to missing a loved one that has died, it is valuable to examine the root cause of the despair. Most people will explain that the cause of such grief is painfully obvious, as we grieve because of the finality of death. We can no longer talk to our loved one, nor can we see, hear, touch, smell or simply share with the person that was summarily removed from our lives. Even worse, there is no prospect of changing the situation. Despite living in a world that teaches us that anything is possible, we are now faced with a situation that is utterly and permanently set in stone, and nothing can be done to change the circumstances.

However, what if we grew up in a culture that taught us that we all were composed of two parts, a physical container that was short lived, and a consciousness part (or soul), that was released when the container was gone? Do you think that knowing our deceased loved ones remain very much alive would affect the way we grieve?

We know from studying ancient civilizations, as well as more recent indigenous tribal cultures, that such belief systems were in place to varying degrees. There appears to have been an inner knowing that has been lost to a great many of us in the modern world. We willingly focus on the external world and could not care less about exploration of the inner world. Even worse, we now have little need to contemplate things that do not result in instant results and gratification. Information can be accessed in a blink of an eye with the click of a mouse, which reinforces the notion that all we will ever need to know will always be right in front of us. Personal human interaction has become expendable, as we spend most of our days looking at screens, whether they are attached to computers, smart phones, televisions, or other devices. Many see few differences between human consciousness and the devices upon which rely. Our brains are like computers, and who we are is determined by electrochemical processes that fire and produce consciousness. In other words, we are what our brains tell us we should be.

But what if our educators, scientists, medical professionals, media, clergy, and family members are wrong? What if we exist in a web of connectivity, not via computers and the internet, but by a consciousness that permeates the universe and connects to realms of information and existence that most can only imagine? Well, despite what you have been taught, despite what you feel that logic impels you to believe, the evidence points to the fact that we are much more than our physical bodies. We are so much more than computers with expiration dates, every one of us has a soul or consciousness that survives physical death, and our temporary physical existence is a mere blip in a continuum of life.

I firmly believe that one's belief in an afterlife can have a profound effect on one's grief. I will go as far as stating that such belief is the most effective form of grief therapy. This is not only my opinion, but one that many therapists have come to recognize as they integrate afterlife concepts into their practices. After all, if you are grieving the loss of a loved one, the knowledge that you will once again see your loved one is the *only* thing that can offer hope and some degree of comfort. I am not simply speaking of vague hope or a heaven promised by a religion that imposes rules to reach such status, but an inner knowing that is gained either by personal experience or through an examination of the evidence. Over the years I have witnessed hundreds of people who have gone from utter despair and wishing to die, to hopeful and productive members of society, all attributing their progression to newly attained afterlife knowledge. I include myself in this category, as for several years I saw no way of surviving my daughter's death. I was drowning in a sea of unrelenting grief and searching for a lifeline that could provide the slightest bit of air. Even while I was investigating survival evidence, I fought every personal experience and consistently attributed each remarkable communication to coincidence, but eventually turned vague hope into belief, and then *knowing*. Does this mean that I no longer grieve and miss my daughter and wife? Of course not, as not having them in the physical will always present a challenge. However, whenever I feel especially sad I can now step back, review what I have learned and experienced, and move forward with the reassurance that my current situation is simply a temporary blip in time.

I certainly recognize that grief is complicated, and we all grieve in different ways. There are many bereaved people that take offense to the suggestion that their loved one still survives. In their minds, since death is final, any thoughts to the contrary are an affront to their grief. They feel it somehow diminishes their loss and the depth of their despair. Many become identified by their grief, and some of these people feel the same way for the rest of their physical lives, refusing to even entertain the possibility of an afterlife. Others are fortunate to have some personal experience that opens them up to the knowledge of life after death. It appears that those who bring themselves to learn, explore, and share are better able to move closer to the true understanding that we exist in a continuum of life, thus exhibiting a different way of grieving.

The focus of this book is on one form of evidence, mediumship, but I hope that some of what you read will move you closer to discover an inner knowing. Mediums have the ability to both heal and break the human heart. Their work comes with tremendous responsibility, so being able to distinguish between those who can and cannot do what they claim is vitally important.

WHAT EXACTLY IS A MEDIUM?

A Medium is a person who claims to have the ability to communicate with non-physical entities. People often refer to these entities as the dead, spirit, souls or discarnates, all referring to persons no longer in the physical realm of existence. Such communication takes place because it is believed that when we die our consciousness (or mind) survives our physical death. In other words, our real self, including our personalities and memories, move on to another type of existence. Some mediums also claim to be able to communicate with angels and spirit guides who may never have been in physical form and whose purpose is to help and guide those who are in the material world. Many mediums also claim to be able to communicate with deceased animals, as animal consciousness also survives physical death. Mediums act as a conduit or channel and are vehicles by which discarnates communicate. They cannot summon any particular entity to make an appearance (although they can ask), but simply remain as open channels to receive information.

Many may differ about the roles that mediums serve, but I believe that the sole purpose of a medium is to provide specific evidence that we survive our physical deaths. Mediums should not be providing their own conscious explanations, opinions, and counsel, at least not in their role as a medium, as it is only the evidence received from non-physical entities that is important. This evidence can take many different forms, but once validated by the sitter (the person for whom the medium is connecting), can provide personal proof that a loved one in spirit form still exists.

You may have noticed that mediums often advertise the fact that they offer other services. Their websites often provide a menu of other types of assistance that they provide. You might see such things as tarot readings, soul retrieval, home cleansings, angel card readings, psychic readings, medium readings, spiritual counseling, pastoral counseling, Reiki sessions, energy healings, psychic surgery, aura cleansing, massage therapy, pet communication, help with legal issues, past life regressions, medical intuitive sessions, and life coach. What is a life coach anyways, and are there cheerleaders involved?

I don't know about you, but my experience tells me that people often get into trouble when they try to do too many things at once, thus the expression "Jack of all trades, master of none." Mediumship is serious business that takes continuous practice and learning. I would much prefer to see a professional medium concentrate on their mediumistic skills, and not try to be all things to all people. Better to be proficient and evidential at one thing than mediocre at a vast number of disciplines. All mediums are psychic, so I understand the psychic work for sitters who specifically request psychic information, but my radar goes up with a great deal of the fringe stuff. Besides, do I really want to know that the medium trusted with speaking to my loved ones on the other side is giving a massage after my session? It is serious business and I prefer that it be treated as such.

THE EVIDENCE

I am sure that many reading this book have visited mediums, subsequently told a friend, then heard "Well, if it makes you feel better to believe." The friend thinks that it is a polite way of saying that you are nuts. I now find such statements to be hurtful and patronizing, as it assumes that one is not capable of discerning fact from fantasy. However, I certainly understand ignorance of mediumship evidence, and the current invasion of pseudo psychics and mediums does nothing to make one aware of such evidence. As you will see as you read on, there is an abundance of credible evidence that some people can communicate with those no longer in the physical world.

As mentioned previously, although this book is about mediumship, it is important to touch upon the other types of evidence that strongly suggest survival of consciousness. Of course, if you believe that who we are is determined by our brains, and that our minds are simply the result of electrochemical processes, there is no possibility of life after death. If consciousness is retained within our skulls, we must be extinguished when the brain is dead. However, if our consciousness (or mind) can extend beyond the brain and not be dependent upon it, then survival of consciousness becomes plausible. What do we mean by extending beyond the brain? Well, telepathy is an example. If we can communicate information mind to mind, that certainly would refute the notion that the brain and mind were one and the same. In the materialistic view of consciousness, how could a physical organ in our body transmit or receive information? Have you ever been thinking about someone that you had not heard from in a long time, and then suddenly got a phone call or other communication from that person? Have you ever had a gut feeling about something or someone that turned out to be exactly true? Have you ever had a precognitive dream that later played out how it was envisioned? It is not clear that such things are the result of communication between two minds, or involve retrieval from fields of information, or are the result of transcending time, but it is clear that something is extending beyond the cranium. There are decades of scientific research that show such phenomena to be real, and those interested in such research are encouraged to consult this book's recommended books section.

Remote viewing is another example of the mind getting information from distant locations, information that transcends the physical laws of time and space. Remote viewers possess the ability to focus their minds on distant targets, sometimes being given only the longitude and latitude coordinates, and then sketch accurate depictions of what they "see." Sometimes they also draw targets from the past that are no longer there, and other times depict targets that will be there in the future and later verified. The U.S. and Russian governments recognized these abilities early on, and all are encouraged to read about the now declassified Stargate Project that used remote viewers to spy on U.S. enemies.

Researchers are starting to amass evidence about distant healing, intention, and the power of prayer, all things recognized by adepts, mystics, and various cultures long ago. These are all examples of mind over matter (psychokinesis), the ability of our thoughts to affect physical matter. Thoughts and intention have been shown to directly influence the growth of bacteria and plant life, as well as processes within the human body. The physical location of the person or persons sending the intention has no bearing on the effects, as distance appears to play no role in thought transference. Such examples of psychokinesis have been documented in the laboratory and have extraordinary implications for changing events on a macro level.

There are many disciplines of research that point to survival of consciousness after bodily death. The study of mediumship has provided a wealth of evidence but is only one discipline of research. Near death experiences have been reported from the times of the ancient philosophers to the present day. People who are near death or under threat of death sometimes report leaving their bodies and visiting other realms of existence. Most significant is the fact that this can occur when the person meets all signs of physical death, including no brain activity, no heartbeat, no breathing, no reflexes, etc. Due to the improved resuscitative techniques developed by the medical field, we are now able to identify more and more people who are able to describe such experiences. They report clear and lucid thinking, which certainly defies the theory that it is the brain that produces consciousness. People report a variety of experiences, such as going out of their bodies, meeting and communicating with deceased loved ones, going through and emerging from a tunnel, undergoing a life review, a sense of interconnectedness, intense emotions and colors, being told to return, etc. There have been blind people who report going out of body during their experience and return to give accurate descriptions of the equipment, including colors and activities that were going on in the operating room. There are those who report being in many different locations simultaneously and are then able to describe the activities and conversations at each location. The research is robust, and the implication is that our consciousness continues despite physical death. Perhaps the most compelling feature common to near death experiencers is the fact that most, after traveling to and receiving information from other realms, return to change their lives forever due to their new perspective and knowledge.

Deathbed visions are perhaps the best example of interaction with those no longer in the physical. If you speak with hospice workers, critical care personnel and some physicians, they will tell you about witnessing such occurrences. However, it most often takes a bit of prodding, as such experiences are usually not readily discussed for fear of the witnesses being judged or labeled. I like to call such experiences a "dirty little secret," as despite being so prevalent they have been kept hidden from much of the public. The fact is that people, in a several week window before death, have lucid conversations with deceased loved ones. The conversations and visions appear to be perfectly normal from the perspective of the dying, but those surrounding the patient usually can neither see nor hear any other entity in the room. The visiting spirit entities are most often, but not always, close family members bonded by love to the patient. The dying person almost always finds great comfort and elation in the reunion, and the implication is that they now realize that they will be helped in their transition. Such experiences occur among those who are receiving medications and those who are not. In fact, it appears that such visions are impeded or prevented among those who are heavily medicated. Often the witnesses are surprised to see patients who are physically and mentally impaired suddenly engaging in perfectly clear and logical conversations. There are some documented cases where others in the room, perfectly healthy people, share the same vision seen by their dying loved one, which certainly eliminates the suggestion that such visions are the result of hallucinations. Although there is no specific research evidence to support it, my feeling is that every one of us will have such assistance as we are ready to move on to the next realm. We may be too physically or mentally incapacitated to express it, but the escorts will appear, nonetheless.

Reincarnation has been studied by scientists for decades. Thousands of accounts involving children's past life memories have been investigated and placed into research databases. These young children start talking about their other families, including descriptive information about such things as their previous occupations, family members, likes and dislikes, habits, details about their home and neighborhood, cause of death, etc. Researchers do detective work by speaking with the children and then trying to locate and visit the previous physical location and families described. Such investigations often involve searches of historical documents, medical records, obituaries, and anything else that could lead to identifying the clues provided by the children. Especially compelling are birthmark cases, where injuries to the body of the previous person (such as stab marks, gunshots, burns, etc.) appear on the child's body in the exact corresponding spots. Once the previous location and family is identified the scientist accompanies the child to meet their previous family, and careful observations and interviews are conducted in the new environment. Very often the previous family is both amazed and overjoyed as they come to realize that their deceased loved one has returned to the physical world.

Sometimes discarnates can imprint their voices on recording devices in a process termed electronic voice phenomena. This occurs on voice recorders, answering machines, computers and other devices, and the devices do not need to be of any special quality. The process usually involves setting some intention of communicating with spirit, turning on the recorder for a short period of time, and then playing it back. The voices are never heard "live" as the recorder runs but are heard upon playback. The messages are short in duration, usually only a few seconds long. Researchers like to classify them regarding their quality, as the messages range from being unintelligible to very clear. Of course, from an evidential perspective it is only the very clear examples that are useful as evidence of survival, and alternative physical explanations for the recordings must be ruled out. Quite often people receive messages on their recorders that are not identifiable as to their origin, but the message is later identified by someone else. In other words, the person in spirit appears to seize the opportunity to get a message through to their loved one through a third party.

After Death Communications encompass a broad spectrum of communications and signs that cannot be explained by known physical laws. They are usually spontaneous in nature, and therefore represent anecdotal evidence of life after physical death. Unlike laboratory evidence they tend to be dismissed as not being credible or subject to replication. However, such personal evidence has been going on since the dawn of man, and the sheer abundance of such communications cannot be ignored. Once physical explanations can be ruled out, such things as unexplained mate-rializations or movement of objects, meaningful synchronicities, electrical disturbances, dream visitations, etc., can be attributed to non-physical sources. We look forward to the day when such things are openly shared and discussed without people being made to feel uncomfortable.

THE HISTORY OF MEDIUMSHIP

Mediumship is by no means a new phenomenon. Some would argue that many ancient philosophers, spiritual leaders, and religious figures gained insight and direction from this practice. Ancient civilizations and cultures incorporated communication with their deceased ancestors into their daily lives. This was not thought to be paranormal or out of the ordinary in any way, as it was simply part of who they were and meant to keep a continuous connection to those no longer in the physical.

During the mid – 1800s, the Fox sisters stimulated much interest by contacting deceased entities that were thought to be responsible for strange sounds, knocks, raps and other physical phenomena in their Hydesville, New York home. The sisters are generally thought of as the impetus for the investigation of mediumship. An era of Spiritualism followed which incorporated non-traditional religious practices with mediumship. The Victorian Era saw the emergence of many mediums, and this can be considered the original explosion of medium practitioners throughout the world. Seances became centers of interest and entertainment among the masses, and major cities housed thousands of medium practitioners. Some of these mediums were legitimate and a small percentage were extraordinary, but the majority were frauds. The proliferation of mediums led to systematic investigations of these mediums by credible scientists, researchers, and organizations.

There are several different types of mediumship. Most people are familiar with only one type, *mental mediumship*, which is the most common form of mediumship practiced today. This refers to communication with spirit through a telepathic process. The theory is, since consciousness survives physical death, telepathy is not limited to those that are embodied. Although the actual mechanism that allows the process has not been scientifically identified, mediums describe the ability to "raise their vibratory level" to facilitate communication with those in spirit form. It is believed that those in these other realms of existence experience higher frequencies than those in the denser physical world. If this is true, it would also mean that those in spirit need to find a way to lower their frequencies to synchronize with the medium. According to mental mediums, spirit makes themselves known to them through the physical senses of seeing, hearing, feeling, smelling, and knowing. Sometimes the process is subtle, with mediums simply describing a sense of presence.

Trance mediumship is believed to be a form of mental mediumship and involves the process of spirit using the medium's mind to convey thoughts. The spirit entity often takes over the physical body of the medium and speaks through the medium's vocal cords. Trance mediums remain conscious during the process but describe allowing their conscious mind to recede into the background as they allow spirit to "take over." There is evidently a difference between light trance where the medium has awareness of the information coming through, and deep trance where the medium may not have any recall of the process or information. Deep trance mediums were popular during the Victorian Era, although in more recent times "channelers" have been witnessed going into deep trance in which they become occupied by spirit entities who deliver messages of deep importance and understanding. There are mental mediums today that sometimes go into trance, but it is not very common.

Physical mediumship also involves a discarnate taking over the medium's body, but includes manifestations of energy that result in observable physical phenomena. This can involve noises, voices, materializations, apports, levitations, movements of objects and a substance called ectoplasm that exudes from the medium. It is not uncommon for people to witness limbs, faces and full bodies formed from ectoplasm, which eventually either returns to the body of the medium or dissipates. Although some researchers claim that the physical phenomena are purely the result of psychokinesis from the minds of the living, others are convinced that it is spirit who produce the various phenomena. All agree that the combined energy of sitters attending the séance is integral to the process. Physical medium sessions often include spirit entities communicating evidential information and spiritual messages delivered to the session attendees. Although there are still physical mediums in practice today, this type of mediumship was much more prevalent in earlier times. In addition, since these mediums insist on working in total darkness, many use fraudulent techniques and scientific investigation of the process is difficult.

Since the mid – 1800s mediums have been studied by some of the greatest minds of science and philosophy, most of who concluded that the evidence presented by some mediums strongly suggested survival. Mediums that took part in such investigations were subject to the most demanding conditions, including extensive body searches, room surveillance, and being bound to a chair by rope and other fastening devices. The list of these scientists and researchers from the past is extensive and includes members of the most prestigious scientific organizations from the fields of physics, chemistry, and psychology. A few members of this esteemed group from the past included Marie Curie (physicist, chemist, Nobel prize), Dr. Alfred Russel Wallace (theory of evolution), Dr. Charles Richet (Nobel prize in Medicine), Frederick W.H. Myers. (scholar and founder British Society for Psychical Research), Sir Oliver Lodge PhD (physicist – patents in wireless telegraphy), Dr. James Hyslop (Professor of Ethics & Logic at Columbia University), Sir Arthur Conan Doyle (Physician and writer of Sherlock Holmes), Judge John Worth Edmonds (legal scholar and member of the NY State Supreme Court), Sir William Crookes (chemist & physicist – inventor of vacuum tubes), Dr. Richard Hodgson (doctor of law and psychical researcher), and Dr. Robert Crookall (geologist and investigator of out of body experiences).

Modern day research of mediumship continues in private research facilities and universities, including the Windbridge Research Center, the Division of Perceptual Studies at the University of Virginia, and other institutions and universities in the United States and across the world.

PSYCHICS VS. MEDIUMS – WHAT ARE THE DIFFERENCES?

I have found that the most people do not realize that there is a difference and believe that the two terms can be used interchangeably. Even people who sat with a medium will later describe that they went to a psychic. You may have heard it said that "all mediums are psychic, but not all psychics are mediums." I believe this statement to be true. There is a difference between picking up information telepathically from the living and communicating with the deceased. The process could involve the same underlying mechanisms, but I believe that a practitioner should be able to tell the difference between the two types of information. There are many excellent psychics who can tell you what color your kitchen is painted, your medical history, and perhaps describe events that have yet to occur, but they have no ability to receive information from those in spirit. When evidential mediums are asked how they can tell the difference, most advise that the information has a different "feel" to it. In other words, not only are the two types of communication distinguishable, but they feel an obligation to advise the sitter when the information communicated is psychic in nature as opposed to coming from a spirit entity. It is only the latter that provides evidence that we survive physical death.

Certified medium Laura Lynne Jackson and author of "The Light Between Us" and "Signs", related the difference in a blog by Dr. Calvi-Parisetti:

While I begin individual readings by linking energy psychically with the sitter (on the left side of my screen) while waiting for the other side to step through on the right side of my screen, I usually don't remain on the psychic side of my screen for long. Once the discarnates step through, I stay on the right side of my screen – so the information I receive is from discarnates and I am reading mediumistically. Again, reading psychically feels very different than reading mediumistically: reading psychically is "retrieving" information while reading mediumistically is "receiving" information. One rule of thumb is that all mediums are psychic, but not all psychics are mediums. I feel that developing one's psychic abilities unlocks or heightens one's ability to connect with and communicate with the other side. Mediumship communication is more like driving on a highway, while reading psychically is like taking a much slower and smaller road.

It is not ethical for a psychic to advertise themselves as a medium if they are not proficient in communicating with the deceased. Some psychics have disagreed, stating that all psychic information comes from spirit. Although this possibility cannot be entirely dismissed, if all telepathic information comes from discarnate entities, shouldn't the medium be able to give some identifying information about the discarnate source? We strongly suspect that phenomena such as telepathy, remote viewing, precognition, etc. are very likely inherent to our nature and have nothing to do with spirit communication.

Certified Medium Doreen Molloy and author of "Proof Positive" provided the following true account that helps to illustrate the way mediums can not only differentiate between psychic and mediumistic information, but integrate the two effectively:

Celeste first contacted me a few years ago…. At the time, she was living in NYC with her three young daughters and was estranged from her husband, with divorce proceedings in the works. She felt that something was mentally wrong with him … and she was very concerned about her safety, as well as the safety of her children. The girls noticed it, too; they didn't really want to go with their father on visiting day – and Celeste thought it was very strange that he only wanted to be with one of his daughters and not the others. This sent her psychic antenna soaring, so she had begun the process of filing for sole custody of her children, but until that legal process was complete she didn't have much recourse. She also had a boyfriend and was concerned that her husband might become vindictive because she was moving on with her life. Her first consultation with me was a psychic reading... as I helped to give her insight into all her options, and we left it at that.

About six months later, she scheduled another session with me – only this time, she was feeling very anxious. Her estranged husband wasn't doing anything specific that she could really put her finger on, but she was constantly looking over her shoulder – and she felt extremely threatened by him. She was also worried about her boyfriend, Rick; she had an awful foreboding that something bad was going to happen to either him or to her. I didn't like what I was sensing either; I felt that her concerns were definitely justified and that she needed to be careful. Once again, we discussed her circumstances and I suggested that she speak with the authorities about getting a restraining order. I had confirmed what she was thinking; something wasn't right.

Eight months later, she emailed me requesting a psychic-mediumistic reading; it was the first time she wanted mediumship included during her session... and as soon as we got on the phone, I realized why. Her boyfriend, Rick had been murdered – shot at point blank range in his apartment... and she was absolutely certain that her husband had killed him. Not only was she certain of this, but the police told her that he was their number one suspect as well... however, they had nothing solid on him. He had a shaky alibi and clearly had motive and opportunity, but without any solid evidence, they couldn't charge him. He lived and worked in NYC – and Rick lived in NJ, near the GW Bridge, but they couldn't prove that her husband was in that area at the time Rick was murdered, nor could they prove that he had travelled from New York to New Jersey, and back again. The Easy Pass and GPS in his vehicle showed nothing... so for the moment, he was a free man.

I also knew that he had killed Rick; I could feel it. I was able to connect with Rick's spirit right away. I asked him to tell me what happened.... He showed me that he had been at home watching TV; it was nighttime and someone knocked at the door. When he opened it, Celeste's husband was standing there with a gun, and shot him twice. He told me that his passing was very quick... I felt that he was hit in the torso and heart... I told him we needed something, some kind of lead, any information that would help the police to connect his murder to Celeste's husband. That's when he did something pretty astounding. He showed me a man's hand; he held it up right in front of my face, only one finger was missing! When I told this to Celeste, she gasped; she said that her husband's brother has a missing finger! It was now obvious to both of us how her husband got back and forth across the Hudson River; his brother had driven him. As I finished the reading, I felt so bad for Celeste… She was grieving for Rick, terrified for her life and those of her children… and was literally rattled to the core at this new piece of information. She told me that she was going to call the officer who was handling the case the minute we got off the phone… but I had no way of knowing what had actually happened after that.

A few months later, I got a phone call from my friend and colleague, Maria… who happens to be a professional astrologer. Some of our clients consult with both of us. She told me that she had just done a consultation for Celeste, and that she told Maria to 'say hello' when she spoke with me. I was so glad to hear that Celeste was okay! That's when Maria told me that Celeste's husband had indeed been convicted of Rick's murder and would be in prison for a very long time. It was a 'wow moment' because I knew that Rick had given us the one critical piece of information that helped to 'connect the dots' and ended up breaking the case.

Celeste has since healed and is now living in Europe with her daughters. She finally feels 'safe'… and can now move forward with her life. Meanwhile, I never ceased to be amazed at what might come through during a reading!

I have assisted in informal research with mediums to try to determine if their brain wave patterns were different when engaged in mediumship versus psychic exercises. Very proficient and evidential mediums were put through psychic exercises as part of the research. My observation was that, at least in this protocol, the psychic ability among most of the mediums was only what would be expected by chance. In addition, over the years I have observed that psychic predictions from excellent mediums have proved to be mediocre in accuracy. This reinforces my personal belief that, despite the assumption that mediumship involves mind to mind communication, the process of communicating with the deceased involves components that have yet to be discovered.

CAN MEDIUMS SEE THE FUTURE?

People regularly have precognitive episodes in which they see future events being played out. This most often occurs during altered states of consciousness such as while dreaming. The theory is that time and space may govern the physical world, but there are no such restrictions in other fields of consciousness or realms of existence. Since mediums are also psychic they often receive information about future events that does not emanate from discarnates, but from fields of information or from the minds of other living beings. Most often such psychic information appears to be advisory in nature, as it includes events that will occur in the future but cannot be verified in the present. For example, if a psychic told you that you will be married in two years to someone you have yet to meet, you would be in no position to know whether the information is correct until the two years have passed. Many people are anxious to learn what the future holds for them, but only if the information is positive. Before asking a medium to provide psychic information, make sure that you are prepared to accept the information that may be provided. Although the information given is usually positive, you may not agree with or want to accept some of the information communicated.

Also, please consider the very real possibility that the future is not etched in stone. The future may exist with many different pathways, and free will might certainly influence the course of events. In addition, we must keep in mind that those no longer embodied also have free will, and thus the ability to help alter the course of direction in our physical lives. The pathway envisioned by the medium may be just one of many forks in the road. Those familiar with the principles of quantum physics might also suggest that our observations, even on a macro level, could possibly bring certain events into fruition. You may wish to use psychic information as a guide, but it may very well be a mistake to make major life decisions based upon what you were told.

Sometimes people who received psychic readings later report back to the mediums after the events have played out. Most times they verify the psychic information that was conveyed to be true, but not always. Also, what appears to be confirmed may be subject to further twists and turns. Certified medium Janet Mayer and author of 'Sprits…They Are Present" illustrates this point quite well with the following account:

At the end of my clients reading I asked if she had any questions. After thanking me she said yes, I have one, "Do you see any more children in my future?" I told her that from everything I received in her reading there was no mention of another child, but I would see if I could psychically receive any other information. I sat for a moment and heard the word "No" clearly in my mind. After carefully explaining that I heard the word, "No" I also told her that of course she could always prove me wrong. I have no control of that, and she should always be responsible if she didn't want any more children and I left it at that.

Months later I received an email from her stating that she just wanted to let me know I was wrong, very wrong, and she was pregnant. She went on to say she thought I should know so I don't tell that to someone else in the future. Although she was thrilled, I sensed fear and thought she was upset with me. My first thought was, "Seriously?" As a psychic medium I know I heard the word "No" very strongly, and I always go with exactly what I hear, and I won't change that. I also know I was being a responsible adult and psychic medium with my response to her. Being human I was sort of bent out of shape and upset that my information was completely wrong, but I had to let it go as I have no control over someone else and their choices.

About three weeks later I received another email from her informing me that she had a miscarriage and that I was right. She again just thought I should know that what was said in the reading was correct. I cried as I read it. She then went on to apologize for sending the first email, stating she was so surprised and somewhat afraid because she has a disability and wasn't sure she could handle it right then, and her fears came out to me.

Tracey also recently shared something more. She mentioned throughout the reading I kept mentioning that Spirit was showing me her feet. There was something seriously going on with them, as Spirit was showing it and I could sense it. She explained that when she was born, the doctors said she would never walk. In the 1970's at six months old she was sent to Shiners Hospital in Illinois and stayed for numerous visits, six months at a time, until she could walk again. She said that the reading has stayed with her because not only could I not have known that she was born this way, but Spirit told her: Your challenges do not define you; you are living the life you are supposed to live in the way that you are supposed to live it.

Sometimes information given about a future event is given to the medium by the deceased. Evidently the dead, who are no longer restricted by our physical laws, have access to information that we refer to as coming from the future.

Certified Medium Lynn LeClere related the following to me (my words):

A woman who was a psychiatrist came to me for a reading. During the reading the woman's deceased husband came through with a great deal of evidential information identified by his wife. He specifically told me that he had a son who was a medical doctor in the Emergency Room, which the sitter immediately validated. He then went on to explain that his other son was "stealing," which I expressed to the sitter, who then explained that this was also true. She related the fact that this son was in the family business and was caught embezzling money from the firm. The deceased husband then went on to describe an event that was yet to occur, where planes would fly into tall buildings and cause mass destruction. He went on to advise that another plane would hit a building in Washington, DC, and yet another would go down in Pennsylvania. This of course could not be validated by the sitter, but she was interested nonetheless. The husband then went on to acknowledge the sitter's grandson, and mentioned that he worked in Washington, often flew, and was known to the family as "Pickles." The sitter gasped, as all of this information was true, including the unlikely name of "Pickles."

About a month later, on 9/10/01, the grandson told the sitter that he was taking a business flight to San Francisco the next day. It was then that his grandmother told him about the medium reading, how his grandfather came through, how he was identified by the specific name of Pickles, and the dire information about a plane diverted and headed for Washington going down in Pennsylvania. The grandson was significantly shaken by the information about the flight he was scheduled to take, and immediately called the airline to cancel his flight on 9/11. As it turned out, this flight was the United Airlines flight # 93 that was hijacked and crashed in Pennsylvania.

After the tragic events of the day unfolded, the sitter immediately called to express her gratitude to me for saving her grandson's life. Of course I explained that it was grandfather who intervened, and I was only the channel for the information.

Even the mediums are often amazed by the power of those in spirit, and Lynn commented to me how the whole scenario was "divinely done."

SPECIFIC EVIDENCE VS. GENERAL BLAH – BLAH – BLAH

M ost people who visit mediums have lost loved ones. That is not earth-shattering information, as why else would one seek the services of someone who speaks to the dead? As you might expect, a good many of those seeking connections are in deep grief and desperately want to hear from their deceased loved one more than anything else in the world. Those in such a state of mind will very often make information "fit," even though the evidence might be non-specific. People desperately need to know that their loved one still exists and will often grasp at anything that might remotely be considered communication. Understandably, logic and objective evaluation often do not come into play. Fraudulent or under-developed mediums understand this human frailty and are shrewd enough to "gain favor" of the sitters in this fashion.

I have noticed that there are various types of non-specific information that come up often during medium readings. As examples, the following are a sampling of some common bits of information often communicated by mediums to sitters:

The medium tells you that your great grandmother is coming through. The medium then asks if you have a great – grandmother in spirit. *Well, of course you do, if she were alive she would be 130 years old.*

The medium tells you that she has your deceased grandmother, who is communicating that she had trouble breathing at the end. *Really? Isn't that what happens to us all at death?*

Now, to really convince you that a connection is being made, the medium relates how grandma was a good cook. *Now of course not every grandmother was a good cook, but I would venture to say that 95% of them knew their way around the kitchen.*

An older male comes through, and the medium relates that she/he sees a uniform and explains that could mean they were in the service or had a job that required a uniform. *The fact is that statement will apply to a huge majority of the population of older males in that generation, and you would be surprised just how many occupations incorporate uniforms.*

You get the picture. After witnessing hundreds of medium readings, I am confident that I can give anyone a fraudulent reading that is 90%-100% accurate. Almost every piece of information I give will be true, but very general in nature. That is not to say that such general information should be dismissed – if the medium receives communication from a discarnate it is their obligation to pass it along. What I am saying is that, although true, such information is not convincing. When we score the accuracy of a medium, specific information must be weighted more heavily than general information. For example, in one of the scenarios outlined above, if the medium brought through great grandmother by her name Isabel, and you verified that indeed her name was Isabel, well that is a piece of significant information. If I told you that grandmother suffered from polio as a child and walked with a limp, and that was true, that is specific information. If I told you that grandmother's specialty in cooking was chicken baked in a paper bag, and that were true, that is evidential information. If it was communicated by deceased grandfather that he was in the Navy, almost drowned in the invasion of Normandy, and was wounded in the right leg, this is specific information that is evidential if verified.

You will also find that mediums sometimes ask questions of the sitter during a reading. I believe that the role of a medium is to provide evidence and information, not to ask for it. Of course, it is important to give feedback to the medium advising if you understand the information that was presented. I recall witnessing a

Warranty conditions

Dear Customer,

The **ALDI warranty** offers you extensive benefits:

Warranty period:	**1 year** from date of purchase
Costs:	Free repair / exchange No transport costs.
Hotline:	0333 323 9710
Phone lines available:	Mon- Fri 09:00 am to 05:00 pm

Please contact our **AFTER SALES SUPPORT** by phone or e-mail before sending in the device. This allows us to provide support in the event of possible operator errors.

In order to make a claim under the warranty, please send us:
- The faulty item together with the original purchase receipt and the completed warranty card.
- The product with all components included in the packaging.

The warranty does not cover damage caused by:
- **Accident** or **unanticipated events** (e.g. lightning, water, fire).
- **Improper use** or **transport.**
- **Disregard of the safety** and **maintenance instructions.**
- Other **improper treatment** or **modification** of the product

After the expiry of the warranty period, you still have the possibility to have your product repaired at your own expense. If the repair or the estimate of costs is not free of charge you will be informed accordingly in advance.

This warranty does not affect your statutory rights. In the event that a product is received for repair, neither the service company nor the seller will assume any liability for data or settings possibly stored on the product by the customer.

| KIRKTON HOUSE® | # WARRANTY CARD | |

NAVY BLUE VELVET SCALLOPED CHAIR

Please contact our **AFTER SALES SUPPORT** by phone or e-mail before sending in the device.
This allows us to provide support in the event of possible operator errors.

03/2021

AFTER SALES SUPPORT
☎ **0333 323 9710 (GB) | (IE)**
✉ **reception@premierhousewares.co.uk**

PRODUCT CODE

708964

SERVICE CENTER

Premier Housewares Ltd.
55 Jordanvale Ave
Whiteinch
Glasgow G14 0QP
UNITED KINGDOM

MODEL: 8808371

Description of malfunction:

Your details: Date and location of purchase: _____

Name: _____

Address: _____

E-Mail: _____   ☎ _____

reading where the medium communicated the name "Aaron" to the sitter. Since the sitter was told not to divulge information to the medium, he gave no reaction to the name. As it turned out the sitter's name was Aaron and the sitter's deceased father's name was Aaron. Not volunteering information to the medium is quite different from confirming information that is correct. However, there is no place for a medium asking questions such as "are you planning a move or a job change?" However, if the medium first identified and was bringing through specific information from your deceased mother, and then stated "your mother is telling me that you are planning a move," that would represent acceptable mediumship practice and could be considered to be evidential.

Perhaps some of the most convincing type of evidential mediumship occurs when the medium provides information from spirit that is unknown to the sitter at the time, but the sitter is later able to investigate and verify. This is significant because it appears to refute the notion that the medium was reading the sitter's mind.

I would also like to address what I call the "message conundrum." Forever Family Foundation conducts a medium certification evaluation program, which is an extensive evaluation of a medium's proficiency in spirit communication. In one of the first steps towards possible certification the prospective medium completes a preliminary application. One of the questions asks the applicant which they believe to be more important, specific evidence from spirit or messages of love. Some of the applicants reply that the message expressing love is more important than the evidence. Personally, I dislike that answer. How is one to believe the message if the evidence does not come first? Think back to before we had "caller ID" and you called someone on the telephone. When the called party answered the phone you needed to identify yourself before the conversation could commence. It is not all that different in the mediumship process. What value is it to be told that your grandmother and mother loved you if you have no indication that you are really talking to grandmother? Besides, I have yet to witness a reading where the medium said, "I have your mother here and she wants me to tell you that she hates you."

Please don't misunderstand, as we know that spirit communication is ultimately about messages, and mediumship is the process by which entities of pure thought and energy in the spirit realm get messages through to those in the physical realm through a third party. However, think of it this way, if you were deceased and in another realm of existence, wouldn't your primary goal be to identify yourself so that your loved one would really know it was you? This can only occur by somehow communicating specific information, information that the medium could not know. Of course, after the evidential groundwork is communicated, then the subsequent messages of love can be believed and treasured.

Unfortunately, there are an overwhelming number of practicing mediums who feel that, once they give the sitter messages of love, their job is completed, and they have been of enormous help to the sitter. In their view, it makes no difference if the message came from spirit or from their own imagination. I find this to be distasteful and demeaning to the sitter, as well as to the legitimate mediums. Fooling the bereaved is not the purpose of true mediumship.

What do you think a medium should do if they are conducting a reading and no connection to spirit is being made? Mediumship is not an exact process and relies upon many different factors. Even the best mediums, although they may not readily admit it, will occasionally have sessions where they are unable to communicate with any spirit connected to the sitter. Faced with such a situation, I believe that the medium should tell the sitter that contact is not being made and offer to stop the reading and refund the sitter's money. The medium should not start communicating non-evidential filler information or messages that are not backed up by evidence. I have seen this occur countless times and do not believe that such practice has any part in ethical mediumship. Please realize that I am only talking about a situation where no evidence at all is coming through. Many excellent mediums struggle as they try to connect but put the bits and pieces together into a coherent fashion, and it is only after persistence that the evidence starts flowing.

I must state that I have also seen situations where the medium is providing solid evidence throughout the session, misses a few things, and then had the sitter request their money back after the entire session is over. Fortunately, this does not occur often, as I would consider this to be a blatant effort on the part of the sitter to "rip-off" the medium.

I have often been asked to explain how a medium could give a very evidential reading to one person, and the same medium totally strikes out in a reading with another person. There are many factors that enter the equation, some of which we previously discussed. I am sure that some of you may have been referred to a medium by a friend who told you that the medium was terrific, only to be disappointed with your own reading. The natural reaction by many would be to think "my friend is nuts…this medium is no good." However, the process of mediumship requires a resonance among the medium, sitter, and person in spirit. If all parties involved are not a match it will not happen. Perhaps this could be a case whereby the spirit does not like the medium, does not resonate with this channel, or prefers communication directly with the sitter. Maybe the sitter is blocked by grief or is focusing only on one particular entity. Or, perhaps the reading that your friend received was not as evidential as they thought.

Despite having been immersed in the mediumship world for the past seventeen years since Forever Family Foundation began, my wife and I had personally sat with only one medium for a reading during this time. It's not that we have no desire to sit for a reading, but since our story could be easily researched, we could not completely trust the information. A few years after Forever Family Foundation began, we did visit an unknown medium (anonymously and paying cash) because of curiosity. What prompted the visit was a discussion we had with a foundation volunteer and friend. Despite the loss of her daughter, she never had the desire to visit a medium. It is not that she did not believe in mediums, but she had some apprehension about the process and feared the disappointment if her daughter did not come through.

As her grief continued without any relief in sight, she finally decided to visit a medium to whom she had been referred. The next time we visited with her, there was an obvious shift in her outlook and personality, and it was as if a great weight had been lifted from her shoulders. She spent a great deal of time with us describing the accuracy of the medium and raving about the experience. We were so intrigued by her experience and transformation that we decided to make an appointment with the same medium.

To put it mildly, the session was a complete waste of time. The medium did not produce one single piece of evidence during the entire one – hour session and used every cold reading trick in the book in trying to give the appearance of being evidential. Later, as we considered the situation, we wondered how it was possible for such diametrically opposed experiences to occur. We came to two possible conclusions. The first was that our friend was in such deep grief and having never experienced a medium before, she made everything fit. Her desperation might have clouded her objectivity. The second possibility was that if a person in spirit needs to come thorough, bearing in mind that we all have mediumistic abilities to some degree, they will seize an opportunity to do so. In other words, it did not matter that the medium was not an evidential practitioner, spirit made this happen.

What made the second explanation more plausible is one detail that I left out. While driving home from the reading with this medium, our friend looked to her right and saw her deceased daughter sitting there with a smile on her face.

How Do You Know When You Are Ready to See A Medium?

This question assumes that one has a desire to visit with such a practitioner. If you believe in "ashes to ashes, dust to dust" and see no possibility of life after death, sitting with a medium would not be among your top priorities. In fact, you might look upon those who frequent mediums with disdain and contempt. However, a great many people are on the fence about the existence of an afterlife. They hope that there is a place that we go when we die but have not been privy to any evidence that indicated this to be true, or even a possibility. Their hope is often based upon blind faith fostered by their religious affiliation.

I have witnessed countless numbers of such people who visit a medium quite reluctantly, some walking away with their hope turned into belief or knowing. Of course, the opposite also sometimes occurs as the doubters receive a poor or fraudulent reading, walking away convinced that life ends with death. I had such a negative experience before Forever Family Foundation was formed when my wife and I visited a local well-known medium not long after our daughter passed. Our grief was still in the "horror" stage and we desperately wanted to communicate with our daughter. Most of all, we wanted confirmation that she still existed and was OK. During the one-hour session with the medium no specific evidence at all was communicated, and we walked away with more doubt and no relief from our grief.

Opinion varies as to when the time is right to seek the services of a medium. Many believe that intense grief can inhibit the process of spirit communication and therefore recommend that a certain amount of time pass before trying to contact a deceased loved one through a medium. Another school of thought, taken from channeled writings, is that the newly deceased may go through a period of adjustment or confusion in their different environment. The ability to communicate with the physical realm may be a skill that takes some time to learn and perfect, possibly requiring the assistance of others in the spirit realm. This seems logical to me, especially when I consider the fact that we go from physical embodiment to entities of pure thought, and we are not dead as we thought we would be. I think of it as people in the spirit realm needing mediums in their own environment to help communicate with those in the physical. "Blue Island," a book communicated by W.T. Stead about the deceased passengers of the Titanic, illustrates this concept.

On the other hand, there are many reports of direct visitations and communications from spirit immediately after their passing. There is quite a bit of research that seems to indicate that after death communication is much more prevalent early after ones passing than in later years. This makes sense, as I would imagine those who are newly deceased would see the urgency of getting a message to loved ones that are grieving. "Crisis Apparitions" appear to be another example of contact immediately after death. In these cases, a person sees a vision of a loved one or acquaintance that is thought to be very much alive, but it is later found out by the perceiver that the person had died.

I am reminded of an occurrence in Fort Myers, Florida, where Forever Family Foundation was hosting a mediumship demonstration. Mary reserved a seat well in advance of the event, not because she was looking to connect with a deceased loved one, but simply because she had heard about mediums and was curious about the process. Unfortunately, Mary's son passed one week before the scheduled event. Despite her grief and shock, she decided to attend the event as scheduled. As it turned out, her deceased son came through one of the mediums with extraordinary evidence that he still existed and was happy with his new environment. The specificity of the evidence was wonderful for all to witness, and Mary walked away with the knowledge that her son was simply in the next room. The bottom line is that the time is right to see a medium when you feel that you are ready and open to receive.

Fraudulent Mediums

Mediumship is no different than any other profession and it is not immune to unscrupulous and deceptive practitioners who prey on others. Fraudulent mediums use practices such as "cold reading" where they look for body language clues. Members actually tell us about past experiences visiting a psychic or medium where they were told that they were under a curse, the source of their present troubles, and for a hefty fee the medium would remove the curse. As hard as it is to believe that people take this seriously, the fact of the matter is that many do and are quickly separated from their money. A friend of mine, an intelligent and successful woman, recently told me about such a disturbing experience. Before she realized what was happening, she had purchased "special curse removing" candles from a practitioner to the tune of $3,000. It is easy for us to look at such experiences and wonder how they occur, but grief is a powerful emotion, and the non-physical world is unchartered territory to many people. Fear is another factor, and I am sure that my friend also thought, "What if she was right about the curse?" Since not many people talk openly about their visits to psychics and mediums, there are often no barometers or controls upon which people can rely.

Skilled psychic entertainers employ "cold reading" techniques, and they are very adept in picking up on slight changes in body language as well as being well-versed in human psychology. Everything from head nods, pupil dilations, and body postures are noticed, as well as sizing up one's age, ethnicity, religion, education, etc. Fraudulent mediums are often skilled in such techniques. They know that they are dealing with people who want connections and that these people are more than willing to make things fit. They also know that their subjects will quite often provide them with verbal information and clues that they can use later. Sometimes they will give out a piece of correct information and then reword it in different ways and present it several more times during the reading, giving the perception that they are demonstrating more hits (correct information). If working in front of a large audience, some resort to a "shot-gunning" technique where they throw out a statement that they know will be recognized by many in the audience. They might say something like "I am getting an older gentleman and feel a pressure in my chest, which means he had chest issues before he passed." This will usually result in many acknowledgments, as this condition is very common and could be caused by a myriad of health issues such as heart problems, pneumonia, cancer, liver, and kidney failure, etc. The medium will then hone-in on one acknowledger and move on from there. I should add that some evidential mediums, while working in a group setting, will give about ten different specific pieces of evidential information, and then ask if anyone in the audience can verify all of them together. This would be evidential mediumship as the medium is not simply throwing out one vague statement but giving a specific descriptive narrative and then identifying one sitter to which it all applies.

I must say that I have witnessed cold reading techniques even among some evidential mediums, whether they are aware of it or not. In a fishing technique, the medium might say to a sitter "I have your mother coming through", then notice the facial expression of the sitter, and pivot by saying "this does not have to be mom, it could be a grandmother or older woman who was like a mother to you, or a mother type figure such as an aunt, or it could be spirit acknowledging your mom who is still in the physical." Or the medium might be reading a group and play the "alphabet game." You have heard it, a medium throwing out among a crowd, "I have an "A" or an "E" first name coming through", and then watching for the acceptances.

The fact is that people in grief are very often not cognizant of the information that they themselves provide to the medium. If you ask them after the reading, they will be adamant that they provided no clues, hints, or other information to the medium. However, after going over the transcript or actual recording of the reading, they are sometimes amazed as they realize just how much information they did indeed provide. It is also common practice for a sitter to hear or remember specific evidence provided by the medium differently from what was communicated. For example, a friend once told me about a visit she had with a medium in which the medium identified her deceased husband by name and communicated the exact cause of death. She recorded the session and asked if I would listen to the tape. When I listened to the tape, it turned out that the medium, in fact, mentioned three initials and seven possible first names, one of which was her husband's name Tom. In addition, the medium mentioned Tom's cause of death as being very sudden. This was true (heart attack), but hardly a description of an exact cause of death.

During Forever Family Foundation's certification process I am often surprised when, after a reading is completed, I independently ask the medium for their approximation of the percentage of correct information that was provided during the reading. I recently did just that after one of our certification sessions. The sitter's scoring indicated a zero percentage of correct information communicated, but the medium estimated that 90% of the information provided was accurate. How does that happen? The sitter was pre-trained in specific scoring procedures, so I trust that she was diligent in her scoring. I also believe that the medium was telling the truth when he stated that he believed he was 90% accurate. Some mediums, especially inexperienced ones, have a hard time distinguishing between information emanating from their own consciousness as opposed to coming from discarnates. They assume that, since the information flowed, it must have been from spirit – after all, they are a medium! They also believe that they must be right even though they received little or no acknowledgment from the sitter. There is an obvious need for training of mediums, as it is much more that spitting out everything that pops into their heads and then holding steadfast that the information is spirit sourced and correct.

Although frauds do exist in the mediumship world, it is much more likely that you might chance upon a medium that is well-intentioned but lacks the necessary ability and experience to receive and communicate evidential information. This latter category includes people who have had some sort of common afterlife experience and then convince themselves that they are destined to help people with their gift.

How Do I Find a Good Medium, and What Do They Charge?

It is not always easy to wade through the quagmire and identify mediums that can do what they claim. Forever Family Foundation and The Windbridge Research Center maintain website pages with links to mediums that have been certified by their organizations. These are mediums that have been evaluated under controlled conditions and demonstrated a high level of accuracy in spirit communication. Of course, there are many qualified mediums that never sought certification, and these organizations can only attest to the ability of those who went through their evaluation process. You may also notice that there are now several organizations, some for-profit, that advertise "certified" mediums. In many cases such certifications are granted to any medium that pays a fee, or receives recommendations from friends, or provides a free reading to the owner of the organization. One should always question the details of the certification process before relying on the information.

Personal recommendations from others who visited a particular medium are also good places to start. However, bear in mind that if a medium was able to connect to spirit for one person it is not a guarantee that the same will be true for you. There are simply too many other factors at work that affect the process. Also, consider my previous comments about people who thought their reading was evidential, only to form a different opinion after evaluating the information in its entirety. Ask your friend if they recorded their medium reading and if you could listen to it with your friend's commentary. Both you and your friend may then be in a better position to determine the true accuracy of the medium. There have also been many books written by researchers who have worked with mediums (see recommended reading list), and you may wish to check out the mediums referred to in their books. It is recommended that you visit the website of the prospective medium to get a feel for their practice and other services that they may perform. If you see any red flags (discussed in other sections of this book), you should factor that in your decision to select the medium. By the way, there are good mediums out there who do not maintain a website, and that is not necessarily a bad thing. Some are simply excellent practitioners and not so concerned about their business pursuits.

People often question why mediums charge for their services. In their mind the work is purely an altruistic endeavor and charging money somehow diminishes the work or the integrity of the medium. Although mediums engage in activities that many consider spiritual in nature, they must survive in the physical world just like the rest of us. They have families, mortgages, and all the other fixed expenses that we all face. Many mediums give back by donating their services to charitable organizations, and I am sure that in a perfect world would like to work for free, but simply find that impossible. Besides, how many professions are you aware of that always donate their expertise and never receive remuneration? The fees charged by reputable mediums vary and are usually flat rates for either a 30 or 60 minute session. Although some psychics advertise their rates per minute, reputable mediums do not conduct their business in this fashion. It is not speed-dating. Receiving the information and putting it into language is a process that takes a while. My advice is that if you should encounter a practitioner who claims to be a medium and wants to charge by the minute, you are probably dealing with a psychic and not a medium that is connecting with spirit. The rates charged by mediums for a one hour reading are most commonly in the range of $100 to $500 for an individual reading (most charge more for additional sitters due to the fact that more spirit entities may come through). Of course, you may come across mediums that charge more or less than these fees. Factors such as reputation, location, and proficiency of each individual medium influence the rates they charge. There are some mediums that charge fees that are substantially higher than the going rate. I understand free enterprise and the medium's right to charge what the traffic will bear, but a practitioner must remain aware of how a person might go into debt out of desperation to connect with their loved one. To avoid surprises, one should always determine the exact fee that will apply before deciding to schedule a reading.

People sometimes ask what I think of mediums who guarantee a connection to a specific deceased loved one. The simple answer is that they should not be trusted. As mentioned previously, mediums cannot command any particular spirit to communicate and the mediumship process most likely involves some sort of resonance match among the discarnate, medium and sitter. If one party is either unwilling or unable, the process does not work. Free will also abounds on both sides of the veil. Every good medium knows that the process is often subtle and subject to factors not always within their control.

I previously addressed the situation where a medium is conducting a reading and no communication is taking place, and how in some circumstances an offer should be made to refund the sitter's money. To my dismay, when we ask prospective mediums what they would do in such a situation, some answer this question by either saying that "this has never happened," or "I would proceed with messages of love." I do not believe the first answer, and the second answer is simply not acceptable. As discussed earlier, one cannot ethically convey a message of love without the evidence to back it up.

Can One Become Addicted
to Mediums?

We have certainly seen evidence that some do become addicted to mediums, as they go very frequently, cannot wait for their next appointment, and get very anxious if an appointment is missed. It is easy to understand how this happens, as mediums are often perceived as lifelines to continued contact with a deceased loved one. However, there are several problems with such an addiction. Going from medium to medium most often results in wild up and down swings as the sitter experiences good and bad readings along the way. As a result, the sitter is always setting themselves up for disappointment. In addition, the complete reliance on mediums stifles the person from exploring their own personal communications and may inhibit progress in their grief healing. There is another thing to consider – if one goes from medium to medium, might the deceased loved one think "Hey, how many times do I have to make this happen before you recognize me?"

I guess the big question is "how much evidence is enough?" If one receives specific and evidential information suggesting that their deceased loved one survives, does that need to be continuously reinforced? For those who crave a "medium fix" there can never be enough evidence. Others find comfort and hope by visiting a medium only once or twice, and never again. Most ethical mediums are cognizant of the possibility that the bereaved can become overly reliant upon their services, and they usually advise the sitter after a reading that at least six months must pass before another reading can be scheduled. Of course, this is certainly not a hard and fast rule and each medium sets his or her specific guidelines.

Forever Family Foundation conducted a survey in which they asked people how many times and how often they visited mediums. The results were not surprising, as they indicated that only a small percentage of people reported seeing mediums more than twelve times per year, and there are fewer who go several times per month. Fortunately, addiction to mediums is not the norm, and the largest percentages fall in the category of going either once or twice per year, or once or twice in their lives.

MEDIUMS AND THERAPISTS

Traditional grief therapy most often does not include the encouragement of patients to continue some form of relationship with a deceased loved one. Instead, mental health professionals tend to focus only on ways to cope with grief. Treatments can include various anti-depressant medications or techniques that focus on separation from the deceased as one moves on with their life. However, more and more, progressive thinking therapists recognize the therapeutic effects that belief in an afterlife can have on their patients. They are starting to realize what many already know, the fact that there is nothing more comforting than the knowledge that our loved ones still survive, and we will one day see them again.

Of course, the professionals that incorporate qualified mediums into their practice as a resource do not necessarily believe in survival themselves. They simply recognize the improvements in their patients, and to them the treatment is not much different than the placebo effect in medicine. Sometimes the therapists could not care less about the truth of life after death, and regard it simply as another treatment tool. Others are true believers themselves, something that is most often recognized by the patient. I'm certainly no expert in grief therapy, but it seems logical to me that the bereaved who are open to the idea of survival, or may have had some personal experiences of their own, find great comfort when the therapist can validate their feelings, beliefs and emotions.

I look forward to the day when more mental health professionals become aware of the evidence for survival of consciousness, as they will certainly play a large role in changing worldview. Mediums themselves should always be aware of the grief implications of their work but should never represent themselves as therapists or grief professionals unless they also happened to be accredited and licensed in these areas. Unfortunately, I have seen an abundance of mediums that do represent themselves as grief workers, counselors, and therapists. They do not recognize any distinction between mediumship and therapy, which is a dangerous situation. Some of these mediums believe that, since they have also suffered a personal loss, they are qualified to practice grief therapy.

Another disturbing trend that has become apparent of late is how some grief professionals have started advertising themselves as mediums and integrate the two disciplines in their practice. The concern here, besides the obvious ethical issues, is how they were trained in mediumship, the extent of their mediumship ability, and their motivation. Also, some grief professionals recommend mediums to their clients, which is wonderful when the medium is well qualified. However, some professionals only recommend friends or business acquaintances that are not necessarily evidential, which can be detrimental to the well – being of their clients.

An example of the healing power of mediumship comes from Certified Medium Janet Nohavec, author of "Where Two Worlds Meet", and "Through The Darkness".

On one occasion a woman had brought her husband to me. As the reading unfolded it was revealed that he had run over his three year-old daughter who was playing in the driveway and was not in his line of vision. I said to myself "Oh My God", what can I possibly say that would make a difference. The little girl in spirit described things that she and her father would do together. The gentleman's grandmother came through to say she had his daughter with her in the spirit world. I saw little girl turned to her father and say, "Daddy, all you ever wanted to do was to love me, you never wanted anything else but to love me, tragedy happened, not your intent, you only wanted to love me."

There it was, dad could not bring her back, but he now knew directly from his daughter that she felt completely loved. I hope my mediumship can always be a source of healing. Though I am the instrument of God's gift, I am often left speechless.

One can easily see how such a message communicated by an evidential medium could be infinitely more effective than traditional grief therapy.

It is true that some people, after having a powerful and evidential reading from a medium, transform their grief in a significant way. They need no additional confirmation and can live their lives in a more productive manner, and that is a wonderful thing. However, large numbers of people report that the therapeutic effect following an evidential medium reading is short lived. This often results in frequent visits to multitudes of mediums as they keep seeking more confirmation.

I believe that the reason why so many people start questioning their medium experiences is the fact that they lack a supportive foundation for belief. One needs to change the way they think about death before significant grief transformation can be attained. This can be accomplished in one of two ways. The first route is to become familiar with the evidence supporting life after death. Remember, mediumship is one of many types of survival evidence. The fact is that it is easy to dismiss one type of evidence as being questionable or simply the result of wishful thinking. However, if one is aware of the strong evidence from phenomena such as near death experiences, end of life experiences, mediumship, reincarnation, after death communication, etc., when taken collectively life after physical death becomes the most logical explanation. All the research and all the anecdotal reports cannot be wrong.

I have found that those who have a broad knowledge of the totality of the evidence are able to accept an evidential medium reading for what it is, without doubt or question, and the results are a permanent knowing that their loved one survived physical death and remains part of their lives.

Why Didn't I Hear from The Person with Whom I Wanted to Make Contact?

I recently heard from a foundation member who had visited a Certified Medium and was upset with their reading. It turns out that she went to the medium to contact her deceased daughter, but instead received evidential information from her deceased ex-husband. Her comment was, "I hated the son-of-a-bitch while he was alive…. why would I want to speak to him now?" I explained that the medium has no control over who comes through, as they merely act as a channel for information. A common misconception is that a medium will always bring forth the entity that the sitter desires to hear from. However, they are no better able to do that now than when the person was in the physical world. Apparently, we all have free will, even in other realms. We must also consider that the daughter was simply busy at the time. If we believe the channeled reports and experiences of those who physically died and returned, there is much to do over there.

So, if your loved one does not come through, it simply means that the conditions were not right. It should not be interpreted as an indication that the person in spirit does not love you or does not want to communicate with you, nor does it mean that the medium was bad or wrong. Also, please consider that the person in spirit may wish to communicate with you directly, is simply waiting for another time, or prefers not to (or is unable to) communicate through this medium.

Some people have many loved ones on the other side and mediums describe the ways in which those in spirit line up waiting to communicate with a particular sitter. Just as it is difficult for us to be in a room where everyone is talking and try to hone – in on one particular conversation, mediums face similar obstacles in trying to identify and make connections to one particular discarnate. Certified Medium Joseph Shiel, author of "Edge of Wilderness," once illustrated this point at an event by asking all attendees to begin conversing with the person next to them. The drone and noise level in the room was overwhelming and he pointed out "Welcome to my world!" We must also consider the possibility that some in the spirit world retain stronger personalities than others and might dominate the conversation. I have heard many accounts from people who had a medium reading where the person they wished to communicate with did not make their presence known, but they heard from others in the spirit realm. However, in many of these cases the person soon after receives direct personal communication from the person from whom they wanted to hear. I am not sure why this happens, but perhaps the mediumship process somehow opens a personal communication channel. In any event, personal contact without the services of a medium are perhaps even more powerful.

Are TV Medium Shows Real?

The mediums who appear on various types of TV shows are most often legitimate and evidential practitioners. However, one must recognize that TV shows are designed for ratings, and ratings only. Ratings bring sponsors, sponsors bring money, and money is the reason that TV shows exist. Shows are highly edited, and hours of filming are whittled down to a snapshot selection of the most evidential communications. Do you think that the show producers will air misses or hits? Of course, we will only be shown the hits.

My point is that, from purely an evidential standpoint, it is impossible to evaluate a medium's performance as a medium within a TV show. Most viewers are not able to discern acting skills from mediumistic ability. We see extraordinary hits, but there could be hours of misses to which we are not privy. It is not unlike watching a baseball hitter blasting a home run on the ESPN nightly highlights. We may think that the player is terrific, not aware that his actual season batting average statistics showed that he was hitting only .150, which means he was successful in getting a hit only 15% of the time.

Another fact to bear in mind is that TV shows are staged. The mediums may not act the same way in "real life" as the way they act on television. On TV they are working in the capacity of an entertainer as they take direction and behave accordingly. I do not want to give the impression that all TV mediums are simply actors. Forever Family Foundation has certified several high – profile mediums that have appeared in TV shows, and these mediums are gifted practitioners who are among the very best in evidential spirit communication. I realize that these mediums have little or no say in the format and content of the shows. The problem, in my opinion, is the perception that the viewers walk away with about the process of mediumship. Forever Family Foundation gets calls and emails from people who visited reputable mediums and claim that these mediums were not evidential. When questioned why they believe this to be so, they answer "the medium got some things wrong," or "I didn't understand some of what the medium said." When it is explained that good mediums have a rate of accuracy in the range of 75% to 90%, the retort is often, "well, the TV medium never gets anything wrong!" There are many excellent mediums that do not appear on TV. It is unfair to judge them based upon an impossible standard, a standard that is only a TV perception.

How Should I Prepare for a Reading, be a Good Sitter, and What About After the Reading is Done?

If you want evidence, make sure that you set the stage to receive communication that you can trust. Try to leave your expectations behind and simply remain open to anyone in spirit that may make their presence known. Attempting to "will" contact with a specific entity may cause you to miss important evidence from others that may have messages for you. I have seen it happen so many times, and I understand it. Heck, I have done it myself. People walk into a reading in a desperate state, silently repeating their loved one's name, and blocking out all other thoughts. The fact is that such practice may very well block out the chances of receiving any information at all.

Many people believe that such practices as talking to your deceased loved ones before a reading, lighting a candle, or saying a silent prayer to the universe may enhance the experience. There is ample evidence that this is true.

A medium only needs the basics when setting up an appointment, and name and phone number should be sufficient. One should never divulge any personal information or give any indication of who they would like to contact. If a medium should ask such a question beforehand my opinion is that you should consider engaging a different practitioner. Some mediums and researchers might argue that telling the medium who you wish to hear from facilitates the connection, and it is only the subsequent evidence that is important. Although this may be true on some level, in my opinion it certainly puts the subsequent evidence under suspicion. In any event, wouldn't the medium telling you who they are connecting with be more evidential to you than if you told the medium who you wished for?

I remember visiting a medium soon after my daughter's passing, and I made the appointment under a phony name. In my mind it was necessary to do this to avoid the possibility of the medium doing an internet search on me before my arrival. I am not necessarily recommending that you do the same when visiting a reputable medium, as evidential and ethical mediums never resort to such fraud or deception. However, the frauds will and do engage in investigative measures before a reading. It is amazing how much identifying information can be gleaned from social websites and internet searches. I recall receiving an application from a perspective medium for the foundation's Certification Program. Among her answers as to how she prepares for a reading she revealed that "I always do a Google search on sitters before our scheduled appointment so that I can become familiar with them." If she admitted that to us, I shudder at the thought of the damage she inflicts upon the bereaved.

People always ask if they should record their session with a medium. The answer is an absolute yes, and I suggest that if the medium tells you that you are not allowed to record the session you should leave. What are they hiding? If you are unable to bring a recording device with you bring a pad and pencil to take notes. During a reading, there may be some information that you do not understand and cannot verify. Also, you may have some confusion after the reading as to what was actually said by the medium and having a recording or notes to which you can refer is extremely valuable in this regard. In addition, there is another excellent reason to record. If you are fortunate to get a wonderful and evidential reading, being able to play back the session when you are feeling sad and missing your loved one can be healing. One other possible bonus to recording a session is electronic voice phenomena, as sometimes discarnate entities can record voices on electronic devices. These voices are never heard "live" while the recording is taking place but appear later upon playback. Some people have reported listening to their medium sessions tapes and hearing the voice of a loved one.

I have witnessed mediums telling sitters that recording is not allowed because "it upsets spirit." Heck, the reason the discarnate is coming through in the first place is to let you know that they still exist. Why would they not want you to have lasting evidence? I have also heard mediums say that "recordings won't be successful" and "it interferes with the process." In these cases, I suspect that the mediums simply did not want evidence out there about the cold reading techniques they were using, or their own inabilities. It is true that electronics are often disturbed or malfunction during medium communication, but that is not a reason to ban the use of recording devices.

Many seem to feel that bringing personal items from the deceased to a medium reading will help facilitate a connection. There are varying opinions on this, but if you bring any personal items from the deceased, always make sure that they are well hidden, as it is in your best interest to avoid giving obvious information to the medium. For example, a medium's statement that he/she has connected to your deceased son would hardly be evidential if you went to the session wearing a necklace with a visible photo of your son around your neck (you might be surprised at how often I have witnessed this). Although some mediums claim that it is helpful to hold an item that belonged to someone now in spirit (psychometry), they should be able to make connections regularly without such aids.

Another common question about medium readings is if there is any difference between a reading that is conducted in-person versus via Skype or telephone. Most people believe that an in-person reading will result in a stronger connection among the medium, sitter and spirit. This is not surprising because most of us think in physical terms and believe that up close and personal is always the preferred method to connect. However, scientific research has found that in all manners of telepathic communication distance does not affect the process or quality of the information. In other words, whether the sitter is sitting in the same room as the medium or 3,000 miles away, the connection will be the same. Think about it, if the person in the spirit realm is communicating to the physical world telepathically, what difference does physical distance make? In fact, most researchers prefer to conduct mediumship research via the telephone, as it eliminates the possibility of the medium receiving clues from the sitter's body language. As such, the evidence received from a medium via the telephone might be interpreted to be more significant than if it had been received while face to face with the medium. Skype sessions also result in the same quality of information (of course, if using video, you and the medium will be able to see each other during the reading).

Reputable mediums do not want you to divulge information to them, as they recognize their job to be providing you with the evidence. However, it is very important to let the medium know whether a piece of information is correct. If the medium gives you information that you deem to be correct, acknowledge this to the medium with simple yes or no type phrases such as "I understand," or "that makes sense." On the other hand, if the information is incorrect or does not make clear sense, good responses would be "I don't understand," or "that is not true." I have witnessed a session where the medium stated that she had the sitter's mother in spirit, and then proceeded to give information from mother for the entire session. The sitter did not have a mother in spirit, but never told this to the medium. If the sitter would have simply stated that the connection did not make sense at the onset, it would have enabled the medium to go back to spirit for more information and save everyone a lot of time and trouble.

Bear in mind that a medium reading can be an extremely emotional experience for someone in deep grief, and sitters sometimes get excited and blurt out a tremendous amount of information to the medium. For example, if the medium talks about you having a brother in spirit, don't respond by saying "Yes, my brother Bill is passed and he was an expert guitar player who left a wife and son when he died in a motorcycle accident at age 23." Would it not be so much more evidential if you simply acknowledged your deceased brother, and the medium communicated these other facts? Giving information to the medium is also not fair to the medium, as it leaves little opportunity for the medium to provide specific and significant information, thus disturbing the process. One can also make the case that providing information is equally unfair to the discarnate who is trying to convince you that they still survive.

It is also common for people to try to help a struggling medium. After all, most of us are compassionate people and we hate to see others in uncomfortable situations. Curb your desire to assist by remembering your purpose in going to the medium in the first place, to receive evidence that your deceased loved one still survives. When you are receiving information that does not make sense, simply let the medium know and allow the medium to go back to spirit for more information. An accomplished medium understands that there will be pieces of information that do not appear to fit, but the good ones are able to overcome the lack of validations by piecing together more clues from spirit.

Some sitters are afraid to challenge the medium, as if saying "no" is confrontational. One reason this occurs is the fact that sitters often feel that this would somehow break the chain of communication. In other words, they feel that this might result in the medium losing the connection to the sitter's deceased loved one. For the reasons already discussed, letting the medium know that information is not correct is helpful to the process, and certainly not an impediment to spirit communication.

One last piece of advice is not to lie to the medium. The following account from certified medium Doreen Molloy illustrates this point quite well:

Linda contacted me via email to schedule a one-hour mediumistic phone reading. Before beginning her session, I explained to her that anyone can come through during a mediumship reading, but in most cases I usually do connect with the spirits that most people would like to hear from. That's when she told me that she had lost a child, and that this was the one she wanted to hear from the most. I assured her that I would do my very best to bring through meaningful information.

As I began her session, I immediately connected with her father; he was a very good communicator and shared a lot of information with me that she was able to validate. Several other people made their presence known as well, but as the clock was ticking I was beginning to feel concerned; I know how important it is for parents to know that their children in spirit are safe, and that they are together with and in the care and protection of other loved ones in the afterlife. In my humble opinion, there is no greater loss than the loss of a child.

So I pressed on, but for whatever reason, I was not able to connect with her child. I felt awful, as though I had let this woman down! This wasn't like me, as I've been a medium for many years and I had never before had the experience of not being able to connect with someone's child. I even asked my Guides to help me, as well as asking her father in spirit to assist and to help bring this child through to me. But I couldn't feel this child. As we came to the end of the session all I could do was apologize and tell her how deeply sorry I was that I wasn't able to connect to her child, although it was not for lack of trying. I heard her hesitate and then she quietly said, 'Well, it wasn't actually my child that died; it was my cat'.

I was floored, not to mentioned, extremely annoyed. No wonder I couldn't connect with her child, as she didn't have a child in spirit! I couldn't believe what I was hearing. I had just spent the last hour bringing through all sorts of validating information, from several of her relatives, while at the same time feeling incredibly stressed that I was falling short. And then she tells me THIS. At a loss for words, I think I just said, 'What?? At which point, she started stammering and apologizing; I could tell that she was embarrassed.

And as a quick side note, I don't connect with animals in spirit. There are many mediums that can and do, however I'm simply not attuned to animal vibration in the same way that I have attuned myself to humans that have passed. People in spirit have made me aware of animals in spirit, and occasionally I'll even hear dogs barking, or will receive other cues regarding a spirit animal's presence. But animal communication is a totally different process, and it's not one that comes naturally to me. However, that wasn't the point…. The point was that this woman had been purposely misleading in her request, and because of my compassion for those who lose children, I would never in a million years think that someone would tell me that they had lost a child – when they did not!

We ended the call and I remember sitting there for a few minutes review-ing the session and realizing that I had given this woman a great reading, and a highly accurate one to boot. I had been right all along! Now, I just had to find a way to decompress. As time went on, I never heard from this woman again, and it's probably just as well.

People often ask if there is anything that they should be doing after a reading from a medium. My advice would be to listen to the recording you made or consult your notes to evaluate the evidence. If there were pieces of information that you could not verify, share this with family or friends who could possibly shed further light on the evidence. Step back and review the statements made by the medium to recognize the significance of the facts communicated and the implications of such information. Discount the information that you know not to be true and reflect to determine if you may have unwittingly provided information to the medium. Be sure to make written notes about the specific information that the medium could not have known. Later in this book you will learn specific ways in which you can evaluate the evidence that was provided by the medium.

While listening to the recording, pay extra attention to any extraneous voices that may now be heard. As we discussed, some report electronic voice phenomena, another form of after death communication. Also, it is not uncommon for people to have vivid dreams that include spirit visitations soon after having a reading with a medium. Perhaps being in such an environment opens one to direct communication. We encourage people to pay attention to such dreams and be sure to write them down immediately upon awakening. To make the process easier, always keep a pen, paper, and small light near the bed for nighttime note taking. Many people that have evidential medium readings find it comforting to listen to the recordings from the session at various times, especially when they are feeling down or begin to question if their loved ones really do survive. Such evidence can be extremely helpful in the grief process.

WILL I GET A READING IF I
ATTEND A GROUP SESSION?

M ost mediums conduct group sessions in addition to offering individual readings. Such groups typically involve 8 to 20 people, but much larger groups are not uncommon. During these group sessions the medium goes to various people as directed by spirit. People unfamiliar with the process expect the medium to go from person to person in an orderly fashion to deliver messages, but that is not how it works. We recommend that those in deep grief should consider an individual reading rather than a group gathering. The reality is that you may not get a reading at all when in a group, or the communications may be very brief. Mediums go where directed, but if you imagine many spirit entities desiring to get through to make their presence known, it is easy to see how the medium might attribute messages to someone other than to whom they were intended. In addition, for someone struggling through their grief and despair, communication with a deceased loved one is a deeply personal experience and a group setting might not be the optimal environment. The bottom line is that your chances of receiving meaningful evidence are greatly enhanced in an individual session with a medium as opposed to a group setting.

That brings me to a subject on which I have a strong opinion, mediums appearing before extremely large crowds of 1,000 to 10,000 people. Quite frankly, I hate to see such events. I understand that mediums who are popular in the media must deal with the entertainment and business side of their careers. If people choose to go see a medium in such a large venue because they want to see a celebrity live, I get that. However, the reality is that a large percentage of the huge numbers of people in attendance go because they are convinced that their loved one in spirit will find a way to come through via the medium, and this is accompanied by large amounts of anxiety and anticipation. People believe that, since the bond of love that they had with their loved one was so strong, their loved one will surely find a way to make it happen. The reality in such situations is that, during the entire appearance, the medium will address 5-10 people. You do the math. In a crowd of 5,000 the chance of getting a reading is about 0.2%. Not very good odds in my book. This means that an overwhelming number of people will leave the arena with great disappointment, no relief from their despair, and possibly more doubt about a world beyond the physical. One can make the argument that just the experience of seeing others have their loved one come through with specific evidence will be uplifting to a certain extent. There is some merit in that statement because logic dictates that if someone else's loved one survives physical death, so does your loved one. However, logic does not always take precedence over raw emotions.

Some contemplate whether their deceased loved ones will want to come through in a group setting. It certainly does appear that some discarnate personalities only wish to communicate with their loved ones in a private setting. This makes sense, as people who were rather private while they were in the physical probably remain so in the spirit world, at least initially. In addition, the messages that they wish to communicate may be very delicate in nature and not suitable for a group event. Or it could be that the discarnate spirit is gregarious, but they recognize that their loved one in the physical is in a fragile state.

Certified medium Janet Nohavec relates the following account:

Countless people come for evidential readings, and although the words come from my mouth I am often left in awe of the connection between worlds. Often, I am left speechless by the dialogue between a loved one here and the loved one crossed over. This happened several years ago here in New Jersey.

The interaction started at a demonstration of mediumship at our Sunday services. A young man who had died tragically came through, and it was evident that he wanted to apologize to someone in attendance. He brought his boots for some reason and identified himself by the name Michael. As I communicated the continuing evidence a woman raised her hand and got very emotional, almost inconsolable, and it was clear this was not the right way to have this communication unfold. The young man, her son, had died tragically, but I felt this needed to be private not public, so I stopped the demonstration and asked her to see me after the service.

I told her to come see me at my office so we could sit together. The story unfolded as the young man who was killed came through to say, "stop blaming my Dad, I would do it again." He was proud of his decisions, and more specific details came through including tattoos, name, birthdays, and other relatives who were with her son in the spirit world. My body hurt from the impact of his death and these boots. Her son had served in Iraq and threw himself on a grenade to save his fellow soldiers. The Mom had never wanted him to enter the service, the father encouraged it. Here he was today, recognizing that his mom was not forgiving her husband for encouraging him to go, and he was pleading with his mom to forgive Dad. He made it crystal clear that he would do this again and felt he had served in honor of his country. He also communicated that his boots had been given to his mom and dad.

The young man went on to speak of the love he had for both of his parents. More evidence came forward from her son. By the end of the reading I wanted to get up and salute a spirit, a young man who had a life and gave it in service. You will never be able to convince me that he was anything less than a hero, a hero I had never met, at least not on the earth plane.

In this case Janet was astute enough to recognize the private nature of the message and took appropriate action. Had she continued to communicate with the son in a group setting it is possible that the vital information might not have been received or communicated with the same impact to the sitter.

Do Mediums Have Different Styles as They Present the Evidence?

Yes, and you will notice it right away. Some mediums are very deliberate and spend 10-25 minutes with each person in a group setting and spend a great deal of time on each piece of evidence in an individual reading. Other mediums exhibit a rapid-fire type of delivery in both situations, giving the evidence as quickly as it is received without spending much time on the meaning or interpretation. Also, some mediums are very compassionate in their delivery and couch their words very carefully. Others throw caution to the wind and give it like they get it, with little care or regard for how the evidence is perceived. There is no right or wrong method, but I feel that the medium should always be cognizant of the emotional state of the sitter.

I find that medium styles are often consistent with their personalities. In other words, mediums that are somewhat shy and reserved in their personal lives often deliver information in the same fashion. Conversely, mediums that are energetic and outgoing often communicate the information they are receiving in a bold and sometimes humorous fashion.

Certified medium Rebecca LoCicero, author of "Messages from Heaven" provided the following account: (warning – this is very graphic with strong language)

In Feb 2014 while at a week-long paranormal research camp I was attending, I had the most personally expressive reading thus far. I was not letting the group that I was with know that I was a medium. It was not my intention to let anyone know until, while sitting with someone, I slipped. Jenny was my partner for an experiment in interviewing. I was supposed to ask a question about her siblings, instead I said, "you have two brothers?" I was correct, but quickly realized that since I "told" not "asked", this might have been suggestive that I was a psychic medium.

Jenny knew at that point and with reference to other situations that I was a medium and when everyone left the room and the class was over, we began chatting. Of course she asked if anyone was around her, and I already knew that a spirit was indeed talking to me, for her, since class had begun. I told her I saw a male with her that loved her very much, a love that is all "kissy" so it was not a relative but a relationship, a male that had crossed for her…. and then…I saw his penis!

How was I supposed to share that information? It was obvious that was the body part he was spiritually showing me "up close and personal" and so I simply said, "he is hanging his dick right out to me!" Waving it around, it's hard and he is insisting that I tell you this, like "look, I'm hard."

She laughed and confirmed "yes, yes this is him, and I know what he is saying."

I went on and shared more of what he was saying. He told me details about how she was his no matter what, but that they were not dating any longer when he crossed. He had a trauma crossing, not an illness. I discussed these details with Jenny, and she confirmed the situation and to whom I was speaking.

Well, it turns out that Jenny's ex-boyfriend, who did die tragically after they split up, was a man to whom she was connected, loved him, and he was special to her. Jenny is a tattoo artist and she tattooed his penis, which had to be hard to be tattooed, which is why he was so blunt and insistent that I tell her. It was the ultimate confirmation for her that it was really him, and it was sooo his personality. I was so thrilled to be able to be so free speaking to her and that spirit was so correct to talk to me like that so I could display his actions and wave my hips and show her vulgarly because he insisted. Some spirits come through with such extreme personality traits, and they will use my human five senses with such energy that collectively it is expressed and in such a humorous and fun way.

I cannot imagine some other mediums getting the same information across to the sitter. Information from discarnates can take many forms, is sometimes very inventive, but always comes with the sole purpose of letting those in the physical know that they still exist.

DO MEDIUMS INTERPRET THE
INFORMATION THAT THEY RECEIVE?

Evidential mediums are trained to simply present what they receive to the sitter. In other words, they should try to let the sitter do most of the interpretation. I believe that where mediums sometimes get into trouble is when they receive a piece of information and then try to make sense of it using their own frame of reference. Instead of simply relating what they see, feel, hear, smell or sense, they often spend a great deal of time describing something that they have misinterpreted in the first place. For example, let's say the medium gets the image of a fire hydrant, which is her symbol for fire, so she asks the sitter if his dad was a fireman, to which the sitter replies in the negative. The medium might then ask the sitter if he was involved in a house fire, which also makes no sense to the sitter. However, if the medium simply said "I am getting a fire hydrant" and asked if the sitter understood this, the sitter might have disclosed that his deceased father bought him a plastic fire hydrant which he loved and it remains in his room to this day.

However, sometimes the medium needs to be somewhat of a detective in their information interpretation. I will give you a personal example from one of the mediums I visited with my family not long after my daughter's passing. I did not know what to expect, but agreed to keep an open mind, as the medium was highly recommended. During the reading the medium identified my deceased daughter and addressed my son by saying that my daughter was showing him a black Labrador dog. This was an obvious miss, as not only did my family not have a black Lab, but we never owned a dog. The medium was quite insistent that this black Lab was important to my son, even though we told him that it meant nothing. The medium then, realizing that he may have misinterpreted the message, asked spirit for more information. He then looked at my son and said, "do you teach karate?" This startled me, as my son was a 3rd degree black belt in karate and did teach. After my son acknowledged this to be correct, the medium went on to explain. The medium himself taught karate to disabled students, some of whom owned service dogs. One of these students owned a black Lab and brought the dog to class. Apparently, those in the spirit world are often quite inventive in their communications through mediums, but it is up to the medium to get the message across.

Certified medium Laura Lynne Jackson provided another example of simply presenting the evidence, and it appears on the foundation's You Tube channel. She was doing a phone reading for a husband and wife, both in their early sixties, and the woman put her reluctant and skeptical husband on the phone. Laura immediately sensed the presence of the man's deceased father, who told Laura that he would like to apologize for the belt incident. Laura had no idea what this meant, did not try to interpret the message, and simply related how dad was apologizing for the belt. As it turned out, the man was deeply moved. When he was a young boy, he decided to embark on a Cub Scout project of making a handmade belt to present to his father on Christmas. His father walked in while he was in the middle of the project, thought his son was up to no good, and proceeded to beat him with the very belt that was meant to be his present. This incident had stayed with the son for his whole life, and Laura was able to witness the healing effects to both father and son as the apology was delivered.

People often wonder how a medium can communicate with a person in spirit who speaks a language that they do not understand. It is a hard concept to grasp if we think only in physical terms, but discarnates are not subject to the same rules and restrictions. Apparently, those in spirit form can make themselves known telepathically in a universal language. One might say that mind to mind communication is the unifying language that we can all understand.

Certified medium Laura Lynne Jackson explains it this way, as posted in Dr. Piero Calvi-Parisetti's blog:

When reading, discarnates often use a different kind of "language" to communicate with me. For example, a discarnate may allow me to "hear" clips of the Italian language (so that I know to say that he/she spoke that language) – but at the same time, the discarnate is giving me information that I fully understand through what I call "thought energy." So, no matter what languages were or weren't spoken, they are always able to communicate.

Certainly, one of the most frequently asked questions about mediums is "If a medium is good, shouldn't he/she be able to give me my deceased loved one's name?" It is a common misconception that mediums should always be able to communicate the exact name of the deceased. Mediums receive and interpret information in different ways, ways that are often subtle. Some mediums are very good at physical descriptions and conveying personalities, but admittedly poor with receiving exact names. It is not like there is a direct phone line or internet connection to spirit. Think of it this way, if you were an entity of thought and energy in the spirit realm and wished to communicate your name to the medium, how would you make this happen? Perhaps, if your name were George, you could project the image of George Washington and hope that the medium receives it and interprets it correctly. Now let us assume that your name is Ilya – what image would you project? You could try to convey an Ilya like sound, but that might be difficult. Or perhaps send the image of an eel, and hope that the medium is swift enough to interpret a name from the image? It ain't easy!

Mediums often receive bits of sounds when spirit tries to convey names, and that is why you often hear mediums repeating things like..." Joe...Jay.... Jon." They may hear one syllable that begins with a "J" sound, but not the exact name. If they are not simply playing the "alphabet game," and have provided a great deal of other evidence, it is important to evaluate all of the evidence in its entirety. If a medium provides 90% correct information but does not get the name, this would still be considered strong evidence that communication with the deceased was taking place.

Professor James Hyslop was a pioneer in mediumship research during the turn of the century. Michael Tymn, a present-day writer and authority on the history of mediumship, provides the following description taken from Professor Hyslop's writings:

"We do not know in detail all that goes on, but we can conceive that a mental picture in the mind of a communicator is transmitted, perhaps telepathically, to the psychic (medium) or to the control (spirit helper). Even though we do not know how this occurs, we can understand why the message takes the form that it does in the mind of the psychic and why the whole process assumes the form of a description of visual, or a report of auditory images... It is apparent that the pictographic process introduces into the communication various sources of mistake and confusion, and thus explains much that the ordinary man with his view of the messages cannot understand. Mental pictures have to be interpreted, either by the control or by the subconscious of the psychic, probably by both."

Another interesting concept is whether a medium can communicate information received from the deceased in "real time." In other words, can someone in spirit describe what is happening in the physical world as it happens?

Certified Medium Lyn LeClere was conducting a mediumship session in her home and provided the following information (my words):

I was conducting a reading for a woman and her deceased mother immediately started communicating evidence to her daughter. As the information was flowing and identified, mother suddenly communicated the word "murder." Since my job is to simply communicate what I receive, I asked the sitter if she had any idea why her mother would say the word murder. The sitter looked incredulous and shrugged her shoulders. It was then that mother continued "someone is shot," and then "another shot," then "another shot," and "another shot." It was as if mother was watching an event take place. Mother communicated that there were four shots, and three people dead. She also showed me that this was happening on the same block on which I live.

Well, the sitter was totally confused and dumbfounded, and said "my mother must be drunk, because I have no idea what she is talking about."

About ten minutes later we both heard sirens and looked out the window. We saw many police cars parked down the block. As it turns out, there was a murder! A neighbor's estranged ex-husband went to the house, shot his ex-wife, daughter, and ex mother-in-law, and then shot himself – four shots fired. His ex-wife survived, but the rest did not – four shots and three dead.

This account is significant on many levels. It not only shows that the deceased can and do observe our physical events, but they are able to communicate the information "live." I might add that Lynn also mentioned that the night before this reading she was walking home and when she passed the house where the murders happened and she had a strange feeling and "got the shivers." That raises the question as to whether Lynn was having a precognitive moment, or the sitter's mom started communicating early.

How Can I Be Sure That the Medium Is Not Simply Reading My Mind?

Skeptics commonly explain mediumship as the process of mind reading and insist that no communication is taking place with the dead. They argue that all the information coming through the medium is either the result of fraud or the medium being able to psychically extract thoughts from the sitter. In other words, if the sitter is there to contact his deceased father and is thinking about him, the medium can tap into this source of information. For some reason skeptics and mainstream researchers find it more acceptable to acknowledge psychic phenomena than to consider the survival hypothesis. Of course, how does one explain the medium providing information that is unknown to the sitter but later validated?

In addition, it is difficult to explain "drop-in" communicators, people in spirit who are unknown to the sitter and medium but communicate through the medium during a session. In these cases, the information provided by the "drop-in" communicator often turns out to be specific and evidential. When we consider that the spirit communicator is unknown to the sitter and the medium, "drop-ins" seem to refute the notion that the medium is reading the sitter's mind.

Another explanation given by some researchers is that some people can tap into a field of information that contains imprints from past, present and future. Some refer to such a storehouse of information as the Akashic Field or Super-Psi. The explanation is that mediums are not communicating directly with those in the spirit realm but are extracting the specific information from this field of endless data. As if that were easy to do! If such a data fields exists how would one extract a personality from such a realm? It is plausible to suggest that one can extract a factual bit of information from such a data bank, but how does one extract a discarnate's roaring laugh, love of art, or attraction to the color red? Personally, I find the survival of consciousness hypothesis to be much more plausible.

As discussed earlier, since all mediums are also psychic, they do have the potential capability of reading your thoughts, but that cannot discount the evidential information obtained through mediumship. Scientific research of mediumship incorporates blind sitter protocol to effectively eliminate the possibility that the medium is reading the sitter's mind. In other words, proxy sitters are used, which are people who stand in for the real sitters. These proxies do not have any knowledge about the sitter or the discarnates but evidential information comes through. I think that mediumship research has progressed to the point where we cannot attribute spirit communication to telepathy among the living.

HOW DO MEDIUMS PREPARE FOR READINGS?

M any people believe that mediums engage in some ritual as they prepare to do a reading. It is true that many mediums meditate before a session as they try to attain an altered state of consciousness to be receptive to receiving information. Some mediums relate that they ask their guides in spirit to assist in bringing through discarnate entities. Others seem to simply relax in solitude as they try to quiet their minds, perhaps lighting candles or burning sage in the process. Some mediums find it helpful to abstain from eating before a reading. However, I have had large meals with mediums before they demonstrated, and this had no adverse effect on their ability to connect with spirit. I have also noticed that many mediums require no meditative preparation before doing readings. In fact, these mediums become quite "hyper" as the energies seem to build in preparation for what is to come. The bottom line is that there is not a set formula to prepare for mediumistic communication. In addition, some mediums receive information from discarnates well in advance of a scheduled reading. In these circumstances the information and communications seem to download into the mind of the medium in a sort of preparation process.

Certified Medium Janet Mayer provided the following account:

"Every medium works differently and because of the way I personally work, I prefer to read one person per reading. That way I can specifically focus on their energy and who comes in around them. However, four days before Marion's reading, I was writing down what I was receiving during

meditation when I heard a Spirit tell me to, "Invite his wife." I stopped and thought, "No, I don't work that way," but again I heard, "Invite his wife." So, I stopped writing and before I changed my mind I immediately sent an email asking my client if his wife was available to be present during the phone reading. Not surprised and knowing the way Spirit works, she was not only available, but she also informed me later that she was planning on being in the other room hoping to catch a word or two.

The morning of the reading for Marion and Lyn, I woke up and kept hearing: Ashes to ashes, dust to dust. Assuming this had to do with a loved one being cremated; I wrote it down to share with them later that morning. It was during the reading that a number of children were gathering on the other side to thank Lyn, which was such a sweet vision, but a couple of young men stood out. One was their son; the other young man just popped in and wanted to be recognized. His energy felt especially strong to me and I went on to describe a couple of things he showed me and then I moved on. Although he felt connected to Lyn, he also felt a bit outside of their family circle.

It wasn't until a couple months later while at the Forever Family Foundation conference that a woman came up to me who I had never met and introduced herself with a glowing smile on her face. She proceeded to tell me that her son who passed came through a reading I did for a couple (Marion and Lyn) months earlier. She continued with her story about how the owner of Star Seed Gems, Lyn, was at the time of the reading creating a lovely pendant from the cremains of her son and he was the one who came through to make sure he was acknowledged. She then held up her beautifully crafted pendant for me to see. I felt honored to be a part of this link. As I walked away I was so glad I listened that morning to Spirit. Without Lyn present, that special connection to this other Mom and her son may have been lost."

Some might wonder whether a medium ever gets nervous before a scheduled reading. Most experienced and evidential mediums are confident and comfortable before private and group sessions. However, I have been with mediums that were very experienced in doing private readings but were doing a group reading for the first time. Some of these mediums were anxious and pacing prior to the event, and they needed some reassurance that the spirit communication would start flowing once they began. Sometimes what we might interpret as nervousness is simply the result of dead people "lining up" as they recognized the opportunity to communicate. One could only imagine the energy which could be building in the medium.

Perhaps a better question to address is whether mediums feel pressure when they work. Evidential mediums certainly recognize that the bereaved desperately want a connection and need to know that their loved one survived death. Can you think of a more pressure-filled occupation? It is a heavy burden to know that you may be a lifeline for someone on the edge. This can lead the medium to mix in their conscious thoughts with the actual spirit communication. I like to call this "filler." There may be a pause in the communication flow from spirit, so rather than sit in silence the medium throws in some of their own interpretations and messages. That is where mediums can get into trouble. It may not be recognizable to the sitter, and some may even find it comforting, but it has no place in true mediumship. I understand why it happens. Especially in the arena of group readings, we have put the mediums in the position of being performers as they try to live up to expectations. We live in a society that expects a great deal from our performers, whether they are actors, athletes, musicians, or mediums. We are often quick to build them up as their career unfolds, but just as eager to tear them down when the performances do not meet our expectations. As such, the medium performer feels the need to keep the information flowing. "Dead air" (excuse the pun) is a no-no on radio, and you do not see people on stage reflecting in silence. However, most often some form of silence is needed by the medium as he/ she seeks to "hear" the discarnate. Mediums are human and they do not like to be perceived as ineffective or struggling, and silence gives that perception. I hope that in the future all mediums and sitters come to the realization that it is the quality of the evidence and not the quantity that matters most.

Do Mediums Speak to Our Loved Ones Directly or Through Others?

The trance mediums of yesteryear communicated with spirit "controls" that would get the messages from the person in spirit that wished to communicate, and then the control would transmit the information to the medium. In this sense the control can be thought of as a medium on the spirit side. Afterlife historian and author Michael Tymn recently provided the following explanation:

"The reason that trance mediums needed controls was that the soul of the trance medium vacates the body and is taken over by the control, and it is the control actually speaking, not the medium, even though the medium's brain is being used. The control is also using the medium's vocal cords. In normal clairvoyance, the soul (assuming that is the word to use) does not vacate the body. Most spirits do not know how to control a trance medium and so the spirit control was necessary. At times, however, the control recognized that certain spirits were capable of controlling the medium directly and thus stepped aside."

In all the readings by mental mediums I have witnessed over the years, I have never heard one medium describe the information as coming from a control versus directly from the loved one in spirit. Many mediums do speak about having one or several guides on the other side, and often ask these guides for assistance before and during readings, but never attribute the information as coming directly from the guide. The use of controls is apparently limited to trance and physical mediums, which were much more prevalent years ago. However, I must say that the possibility that our loved ones on the other side need assistance in learning how to communicate with the physical world makes sense to me. Just think about the life adjustments that we must make here when moving to a new location. Imagine what it must be like adjusting to a new dimension. The good news is that we apparently have guidance and helpers in the new realm.

Do Mediums Get Signs Like the Rest of Us?

As discussed earlier, signs from the deceased are a broad category that encompasses many types of phenomena. They can take the form of dream visits, physical manifestations (movement of objects), energy manipulations, apparitions, synchronicities, apports (the appearance of material things), and a host of other communications that one cannot attribute to physical sources. If those in the afterlife are entities of pure thought and energy, it is not illogical to assume that they can harness their energy in ways that defy materialist thinking. Mediums are people too, and sure they receive signs like the rest of us, only sometimes more profound. These signs are ways in which our loved ones can not only let us know that they still exist, but also take an interest in our lives in the physical.

This is how Certified Medium Janet Mayer explains it:

"I have an angel statue that sits on my desk and has never moved in over ten years, that is until the day before Damon's reading. Finishing my meditation and writing up my notes for my client, Marisa, I put them away and left my office. When I returned later that day, I noticed my angel had moved. Being realistic, I chalked it off to possibly hitting the heavy desk when I got up, although it's not very plausible with the desk being extremely large and heavy. Although my angel has never moved in the past, I moved her back in place, facing me and went about my day wondering in the back of my mind if I had a visitor.

The following morning when I walked into my office, again the angel had moved. It was very exciting because before I went to bed, I even checked to make sure she was in the same place. As I moved her back into place, I sat down to meditate one more time before the reading. I suddenly felt a young man's presence standing in the office with me. I now knew who moved my angel.

Marisa's son, Damon came through her reading very strong and although Marisa was extremely skeptical at first, it was the information given to her about her son's passing that set her mind and heart at ease. I knew that what I was about to tell her next wasn't something to be given or taken lightly and it's not something I would have ever said if I didn't have the proof to back it up. I told her that I felt Damon was letting me know that he had the knowledge and energy to be able to move, manifest or use electricity to let her know he was around. He also said he was going to show her, and soon. I was so sure he would do this; I wouldn't have been surprised if my angel on the desk moved while we were speaking.

A couple of months after the reading I received an email from Marisa telling me that her daughter was in her bedroom and glanced out into the hall where she saw the night light in Damon's room flicker on while Marisa and her husband Kevin were in the other room having an intense and loud debate. Their daughter Devin, knowing Damon never liked when anyone's voice was raised, ran into Damon's room and sat staring at it. She called her parents in and while sitting there asked, "Damon, are you here?" and the night light flickered off and on. She then asked, "Are you ok?" And it flickered off and on again. They checked the bulb to make sure it wasn't loose and it was fine. They continued to turn the night light on in his room every night, just in case he wanted to drop in. Eventually Damon's night light bulb burned out and they replaced it, wondering if they would ever hear from him again.

When I was asked if I had a story to contribute, I knew Damon's story would be perfect, so I decided to contact Marisa to see if she would mind if I shared her story. As I walked into my office that morning I noticed the angel had moved. I was surprised, to say the least, and had to smile since it had only moved one other time since I spoke with Marisa. I turned on the computer so I could quickly shoot off an email to her and when I pulled my emails up, there was one from her. She beat me to it! She said she was thinking of me and wanted to drop me an email. I responded and asked if she would mind if I shared her story. She asked me to call her and so I did.

She proceeded to tell me that her Stepdad had passed four days earlier and although Damon's night light hasn't flickered on and off since they changed the bulb, it flickered off the night he passed. She wanted to tell me that she knew Damon was leaving her a sign. I agreed. I felt it was his way of letting her know her stepdad arrived safely, and they were together. I followed up with my story of the angel moving that morning and we both smiled knowing Damon was still around watching out for her and the family… and knowing he could contact me if he needed too."

It appears that those is spirit are not limited to thoughts alone when trying to communicate and let us know that they still exist. Psychokinesis (mind affecting matter) prevails regardless of the fact that one of the parties no longer has a physical body.

DO MEDIUMS ACTUALLY SEE THE DECEASED THAT THEY ARE BRINGING THROUGH?

Sometimes they do, as mediums receive information in a variety of ways. Most mediums do not regularly see a vision of the communicating spirit, but it happens. The clarity of the vision can range from a nebulous type of shadow to a clear-cut image that looks just as the deceased person appeared when they were in the physical.

Certified medium Janet Mayer provided the following example – please excuse the language but I felt it important to leave it exactly as she wrote it:

When I sit down to meditate for a reading, I close my eyes and envision the client, who I have never met, sitting in a chair in front of me. Depending on where a Spirit comes in, it shows me how they are related. If they are behind them they are a parent or Aunt/Uncle, on the side a Brother/Sister and so on... However, on this occasion as I sat down to meditate a head suddenly appears in front of me. I have to say I actually jumped and it left me a little off balance. I usually see a Spirit form, a shadow, sometimes a full body, but in this case I only saw a head and it was moving, bobbing a little back and forth. It was pretty bizarre, even for me. After getting past my fear of seeing just a head, I began to focus and try to see if I could get more. I felt I was looking at a male and his energy was sending off an arrogant attitude. I decided to ask "him" if he could please give me more information, after all, how can I possibly tell a client that I only see a head. It was then I heard, "That's all you need, she'll know who I am." Not wanting to argue with a

Spirit but at a loss, I again asked, "C'mon man, show me something!" And suddenly I saw a middle finger point to his forehead and then I heard this sort of smirky laugh and he disappeared. Ok, I guess I'll just go with that, I had no other choice. He has something on his forehead and he comes across with an, "I don't really care what you think, this is what you're getting," attitude. Yikes! I have to say, although I try to never judge anyone, this guy was a piece of work! I wrote it down and moved on hoping this made sense.

As the reading began, I tried to gingerly bring up the man who only showed me his head. I cautiously began explaining the head that appeared to me, type of hair I was seeing and that I thought he had brown eyes. He impressed upon me that the client would know exactly who he was. He also pointed to his forehead so I know he has something on his forehead and with that the client yelled, "Oh my God!" and began laughing. That wasn't the response I was expecting to say the least. It took a couple of minutes for her to stop laughing and explain. She informed me she did in fact know exactly who it was. It was a friend of hers and he had a huge expletive tattooed across his head, (FUCK YOU), to be exact. At the funeral the family was trying to cover his forehead with his hair hoping to hide it, but it was pointless because it was so big. It made for a very colorful funeral. So, this spirit was right, and a reminder that who am I to judge what a client will need or understand? He got his message across that he was ok and the client had a good laugh. And that is why I always give what I get, you just never know!

You can't make this stuff up, folks! People in spirit always have to find ways to provide evidence that they still exist, and some ways are more creative than others.

Janet related another account that incorporates both the vision of the deceased and evidence that the person in spirit is aware of family events in the physical:

Shyanne, the daughter of my client came through with validating information throughout the reading, yet it was a simple gesture at the beginning that meant the world to her Mom. She started off by sending her mom, Sylvia, a huge hug. This wasn't just any hug; it was arms stretched out wide and with a smile on her face. I also noticed that she showed me she was wearing red and I was told that Sylvia has a picture to validate this. Shyanne also showed me that her mom would be possibly taking a trip to China, to which

Sylvia answered she was leaving in three weeks! Shyanne said to let her know she was going with her! Sylvia informed me that her daughter always wanted to take a trip to China, so it was perfect.

Right after that I had a sense of Sylvia getting a possible toe injury and bleeding was involved, so I ask her to please be a little extra careful. After the trip Sylvia informed me that while in China she was pulling her luggage off the bus and hit her foot, her toe to be exact and it bled like crazy. She said it took a really long time to get the bleeding to stop. She also later sent me a picture of Shyanne with her arms outstretched, wide open and a huge smile on her face. Oh, and she was wearing red too!

Most often visions of deceased loved ones manifest in dreams or fleeting glimpses. However, apparitions have been manifesting through the ages, and when seen often result in powerful assurances to the perceiver. Usually those in spirit are not able to manifest in physical form, but can imprint images into our minds, images that we recognize and understand.

Will Bad Things Come Through
During My Reading?

It is a common question that people ask before they sit with a medium for the first time, especially among those who have been taught that they are vulnerable to both good and evil forces. We are taught to fear the unknown, and communication with the dead certainly fits into this category. This is further complicated by beliefs that communication with the dead is forbidden, violates religious doctrine, and will have serious repercussions.

In all the readings that I have witnessed I have never heard the medium bring through dark or disturbing information. This has puzzled me over the years, as it was not what I expected. This book is not intended as a forum for discussion about good versus evil in the afterlife. We all know that negative energy exists in the physical world, and it sometimes seems as if it is dominant. However, the consensus is that we create our own environments in the afterlife by way of our self-judgment, and there is a continuous process of growth. We also suspect that evil people, once transitioning to the afterlife, retain certain beliefs and attachments to the physical world. Their progression takes place at a slower pace than others in the afterlife realm. So, is it possible for a dark entity in spirit to communicate with a medium? I would think so, and I have asked countless mediums why such information does not manifest in their readings. Most mediums advise that before each reading they take specific steps to prevent this from happening. They describe the process by which they ask their guides or ask the universe to surround them with light and prevent such negative energy from penetrating this light. I do not know if this is the process that works, but dark information does not seem to be communicated in readings. I am also open to the possibility that mischievous souls in the afterlife realm, those who retain certain attachments to the physical realm, might not communicate through mediums but choose to try to directly affect certain physical beings.

Perhaps in a dimension where the prevailing energy consists of love and compassion, negative information is difficult to be communicated through a third party. Perhaps the majority of those in the spirit realm progress more than we think. There is evidence for this, as I have witnessed many readings where sitters were apprehensive before the session, anticipating that a relative who treated them badly in the physical might come through. However, invariably when such a spirit does communicate through a medium, the message comes from a changed perspective, one of love, repentance, and forgiveness. One other thought to consider: perhaps what we think of as evil or malevolent in the physical plane might be viewed as purposeful in the spirit realm. My sense is that spiritual growth is part of the plan on both sides of the veil.

CAN MEDIUMS "TURN OFF" SPIRIT COMMUNICATION?

According to the mediums, yes, they can. Their physical lives would certainly be chaotic and troublesome if they were receiving spirit communication 24/7. One can only imagine what it would be like to have endless numbers of entities trying to get through at the same time. Mediums open to receive communication in different ways, including meditation, focus, or setting their intention. When not going through their individual processes preparing to receive, they describe being closed to spirit contact. This enables them to navigate their daily lives in a somewhat "normal" manner. However, I have been with mediums on many occasions in social settings when spirit unexpectedly gets through to the medium, so apparently, they are never absolutely closed for business. I suppose there are very persistent and energetic folks in both the spirit and physical worlds.

I have also come upon many budding practitioners over the years that have not yet developed the ability to close themselves to such communication. This is most often very troubling to the practitioner and can have debilitating effects on their physical lives, affecting their relationships and mental well-being. It is important for such people to seek the guidance of accomplished mediums and teachers who can provide the proper counsel and techniques to avoid this conflict. While we are on the subject, I wonder how many non-mediums in the world, those who possess significant intuitive ability, are misdiagnosed by mental health practitioners who are uninformed about non-physical communication.

For most of us, shutting down from receiving information from non-physical sources is not an issue. Our intuitive abilities are not developed to the point where we can get overloaded. One theory is that our brains act as filters for such information, and one of its purposes is to allow only bits of such information to be absorbed at one time, thus enabling us to conduct our physical lives. I sometimes wonder if it was always like this, as perhaps the ancients needed no such filters, and continuous integration with unseen forces was simply part of who they were and part of the design. However, for highly developed mediums, moderating the flow of intuitive information is both necessary and vital to their well-being.

Certified medium Angelina Diana gives the following account regarding being open to receive communication:

I always try to strike a balance in my life so I can be the strongest for my clients and good for my personal life. I do this by making an effort to close down on my abilities so I am not picking up on spirit that cannot be validated. I tend to open up when I have scheduled appointments. However, sometimes spirits and the bond of love can be so strong that they have to come through.

I was relaxing "off duty" in a bath. I was very peaceful and daydreaming, which is the state I am in when I read for clients. I felt connected to a man. I felt immediately embarrassed because ... well, I was bathing. I asked spirit to connect to me again when I had a scheduled appointment with their living loved ones. Despite this request this guy simply wouldn't go away. I heard him say his name was Ernie. I said, "okay Ernie, I will give you a few minutes, why are you connecting to me now?" He said, "Just tell my son it's okay that he gives away my fishing gear to my friend." I told him I would comply, and he went away.

I usually don't receive messages off duty. Again, I try to balance my life and when I am connecting. I feel I am better for my clients and honoring the messages of the other side. So, I trusted spirit in this case that there must be a reason why this father needed to contact his son. Later in the afternoon I received a call from my sister. She was rather distressed because she had just heard that her boyfriend's dad just passed away. She was distressed because she had just started this new relationship with her boyfriend and was uncertain how to act during the wake. She was calling to ask if I would go with her for emotional support. I felt honored and agreed.

The next day I drove to the funeral home and protected myself so I would not connect. I do this every time I go to a wake. I also wanted to be with my sister and felt that it would be inappropriate to read people not knowing if they were open to what I do. As I approached the guest registry it read "Please sign in and feel free to leave your thoughts and memories on Ernest." Oh My Gosh! I opened it, signed it with my mind racing and said "Okay Ernie…. I guess that I need to find an appropriate spot to deliver this message about the fishing gear.

I entered the mourning room and my sister locked eyes with me. She was nervous but relieved to see me. She brought me over to her new boyfriend. My head was racing with different scenarios as I thought things like "Gee, so nice to meet you for the first time. By the way, your father paid a visit to me while I was bathing."…. err no. Or, "So nice to make your acquaintance, did your dad have a habit of interrupting you while you were bathing"…. Uugghh, no, that would be not be right. I sent a wish to spirit that they would find a way to help me deliver the message. I did not know her boyfriend, and I didn't even know if he even believed in an afterlife. Also, he was grieving and I needed to respect his space.

Before I could extend my hand, my sister said…"David here is my sister Angelina… she is a medium and she talks to dead people." I winced as she said this and all I could mutter was "Um, hi David I am so sorry for your loss." He looked at me and said, "Are they okay, the people you talk to?" I said "yes, actually you might not believe this, but I had a visit from an Ernie yesterday." He looked at me with a mixture of doubt and a smidge of hope. I said, "may I share what he said?" David nodded yes. "He said that it is okay that you gave the fishing gear to his friend." David blinked and said "Oh my god! I just did that this morning! I felt a little guilty because that was our thing, fishing, but I haven't done it since he got sick"

I smiled and just felt honored that spirit did their work. David seemed a bit more peaceful. He then took me to the back of the room to show me pictures of him and his dad fishing.

Spirit always finds a way to connect us. They are always trying to bring us together to remind us that they are still with us. There is always an opportunity for us to connect to them, but we still live in a physical world that demands us to pay attention to the physical life we are in. We need to live our physical lives and they know that. But when the current of love is so strong, in this case the love between a father and son, it needed to be heard. Ernie honored me by pushing me to see, hear and feel his message. This needs to be seen as the wonderment of the love and bond between a father and son and the medium is simply the messenger. They are with us and it's the love that keeps us connected.

The subject of hearing voices and controlling non-physical communication is an interesting one. As a matter of fact, researchers at the Yale School of Medicine are currently involved in a research study to determine, among other things, if those who are diagnosed with a mental illness due to hearing voices might be helped by learning how mediums are able to control such communications. As an Advisory Board member of this study I look forward to the completion of this project and the possible advances in medicine that might unfold.

CAN I GO TO A MEDIUM TO SEEK JUSTICE?

A few years back there was a short-lived TV show involving a medium. The premise of the show was that people who had unresolved issues involving a deceased loved one would appear before the medium, who would take on the role of a judge. The medium would consult the person in spirit and subsequently render his decision, as if in a courtroom. For example, it could be children arguing about dad's will, a loved one wondering about the circumstances about their relative's death, etc. The medium involved was a very good practitioner, but I always thought that the premise was silly, for several reasons.

Mediums are the first to tell you that they very often cannot connect with a requested spirit {there are no afterlife subpoenas}, as they act only as channels through which discarnates communicate. It is more likely that it is the person in spirit who finds the conduit, and the medium cannot force it to happen. In addition, I believe that if a discarnate wants to get an important message through, he/she will find a way and the communication is most often direct in nature, not through the services of a professional medium.

I am reminded of an account in Diane Arcangel's book "Afterlife Encounters." She tells the story of Beverly, whose son Tommy was murdered one winter day. The police notified Beverly that although Tommy was murdered, the body was transported from the crime scene and they had no evidence at the time to lead them to the murderers. That night Tommy appeared to his mother in a dream, and told her that she must go to Brooklyn, and gave her an exact street name and intersection. He went on to say that she would see his blood droppings on the snow at the scene of the crime, and also expressed the urgency of going immediately before the snow started to melt and take the evidence with it. Beverly told her other family members about Tommy's visit, but not unexpectedly her family told her that she was either crazy or not thinking straight because of her grief. However, Beverly knew what she experienced, and decided to head for the crime scene immediately. At the exact location described, Beverly located Tommy's blood on the snow. Of course, she knew that she had a dilemma. If she told the police that her dead son came to her to provide the location of the crime, she would most likely be ignored. Instead, she told the police that she received an anonymous tip and went out to investigate. The police arrived, collected the blood evidence, and the subsequent DNA tests led to the identification of three eyewitnesses to the murder.

Perhaps we should think of events like these, not as cases of revenge, but of due justice, or karma. Revenge could be a human term to describe an emotion that does not exist in the spirit realm. There may be certain issues that the spirit realm determines must be answered for the betterment of mankind. This would have more to do with spiritual growth than the physical concept of revenge. In addition, perhaps many questions surrounding someone's death are not meant to be answered, as they are irrelevant in the "big picture" and actions could result in negative consequences.

Qualified mediums often play an important role in helping the bereaved, and sometimes the clues that they provide can lead to justice as we think of the term. Mediums have also been known to work with law enforcement in this regard. However, I suspect that a form of justice continues in the afterlife as a self-induced process based upon our previous thoughts and actions. Near death experiencers and channeled reports suggest a process of self-justice. In other words, a required self-examination of our actions provides the checks and balances needed for a continuum of progression. We are designed to feel the negative effects that we may have inflicted upon others, in addition to the positive effects of compassionate deeds, and our starting point of existence in other realms is affected accordingly. This would provide opportunities for growth and learning for all as our souls move toward the path of love and compassion.

Seeking revenge for personal motives may not be something of which spirit wants to be involved. Perhaps such things happen only when a positive outcome of learning and growth is perceived. Sometimes, instead of seeking information from mediums for our own personal motives, we might be better suited to remain aware of our own inherent ability to use our own "non-local" senses, those that allow our minds to act independently of our physical bodies, to solve many problems that seem insurmountable.

Why Do Mediums Seldom Describe What the Afterlife Is Like?

This is a common query and one that I pondered myself. If mediums spend a good part of their time connecting with those in the afterlife, why is it that they rarely provide the sitter with descriptions of the realm in which their loved ones reside? After all, descriptions of what life is like in the spirit realm are something that most people yearn to hear.

The fact is that trance mediums of yesteryear frequently did channel very descriptive information about life in the spirit realm. Discarnate entities took over the medium's body and voice and described things such as the environment, thought manifestations, travel, places of learning, etc. By use of this method spirit entities described so much information about the afterlife that the transcriptions were published as books. The trance mediums usually were totally unaware of the information that was coming through, and simply let spirit take over the body and voice. Such mediums often employed automatic writing, where they held a pen on paper and spirit did the rest.

Mental mediums of today are focused purely on the evidence, and it seems logical that this same evidence would be the primary goal of the discarnate. What could be more important than letting loved ones know that you survived death and are more alive than ever? Instead of afterlife descriptions, the discarnates often communicate such comments as "It's better here," or "all is healed." The deceased often portray images of themselves in a healed or younger state as they try to communicate the fact that, not only do they continue to exist, but do so in a better environment. One must also consider the fact that afterlife descriptions will be hard for us to understand, as they do not conform to the physical laws governing our physical existence. Besides, it must be hard enough imparting evidential information to the medium, let alone communicating long descriptions of life in their realm. I must add that there are some mental mediums that do sometimes provide descriptions of the afterlife environment. Such descriptions, unlike the specific evidence they convey, may be filtered by the medium's own culture, beliefs, and orientation. Since there is no way of validating the information it would not fit into the category of evidential communication.

Descriptions of the afterlife are available by reading many significant accounts from near-death experiencers, those who travel to these spheres and return to tell us all about it. There are also many books available that contain channeled accounts describing the afterlife (see recommended books section at the end of this book). The consistencies among the various afterlife descriptions are very interesting and compelling.

Is it Wise to Return to the Same Medium?

There is not an absolute answer to this but remember that it is all about the evidence. The process of mediumship involves specific evidential information communicated from a discarnate entity which could not be reasonably guessed or inferred. Although qualified mediums most often do not recall the specifics of every reading they conduct, it is possible that some aspects of your reading will be remembered by the medium and repeated. In such cases it is difficult for the sitter to determine if the medium is truly making new contact with the person in spirit. Of course, in a repeat visit to the same medium new evidence might be revealed. However, if it is the pure evidence that you seek, it may be prudent to seek the services of a different qualified medium, especially if there is a short time frame between readings. On the other hand, if you trust the medium from a prior reading, and the comfort of a connection is all you seek, there is nothing wrong with visiting the same medium.

I can certainly understand why someone would feel the need to sit with the same medium, especially if the medium were able to provide significant information when connecting to your loved one in spirit. A bond between the sitter and medium might be formed, and one might believe that their loved one desires to communicate only through this one medium. Also, some might fear that they are opening themselves to possible disappointment with a different medium, as there is never a guarantee that a specific connection can be made.

However, research shows that if your loved one can communicate through one medium, the chances are excellent that such a connection can also be made through another medium. Personally, I would much rather have my deceased loved ones come through multiple sources than only one. It is my nature to question one source, but independent corroboration through multiple channels provides the assurance that I need. Perhaps those in spirit feel the same way.

Am I Supposed to
Become a Medium?

This is an important question, as it directly reflects upon the main thrust of this book. I cannot repeat enough the fact that we all possess the ability to communicate "non-locally" with the use of senses that often remain unused. The fact is that people receive after death communication frequently, in different ways and despite one's cultural or religious beliefs. The best mediums are those who have cultivated and honed their abilities to the point where they can communicate with discarnate entities on a consistent basis, with both grace and compassion. They have also learned to present this evidence from spirit in a manner that can be easily understood. Most qualified mediums also seem guided in delivering the information in such a way that those in grief will find most meaningful.

What we have found is that some people, especially after suffering the loss of a loved one, interpret the after death communications that they receive as a sign from the universe, or their loved one, that they themselves are meant to be a medium. This often follows a visit to a medium where they are told that they have intuitive abilities of their own. While this information might be true, the sitter often interprets this validation as an indication that they must develop their own mediumship skills. I do not mean to be cynical, but this often results in the sitter paying for and taking mediumship development classes with the same medium who told them they needed such development.

There are also those who occasionally exhibit intuitive abilities while in the company of friends or family. Since so many people are unfamiliar with the fact that we are intuitive by nature, this often results in the person being told something like "wow, you should become a psychic/medium." This can result in the person thinking that they can do this professionally with a little help, make a good living, and be just like so and so on TV.

The point is, if you are meant to be a medium you will probably recognize this by an inner knowing. Mediumship is very serious business, and the responsibilities are enormous. Sitting with bereaved people, some in very fragile states and wondering if it is possible that their loved ones survive, is an endeavor that can result in more harm than good. Before embarking upon such a path people are encouraged to conduct serious self-exploration to determine if this is truly an undertaking they wish to pursue, or simply a reaction to their own search for meaning after the death of a loved one. Forever Family Foundation gets inundated with calls from people who claim that they are meant to be a medium. As a matter of fact, some of them will start reading the person that answers the phone in the office, evidently an effort to impress with their ability. Besides the fact that an ethical medium should never force themselves upon anyone, the information they communicate is usually non-evidential and useless.

There are many ways to help the bereaved and people in need, and mediumship may not be the ideal pathway to follow. The realization of our own intuitive abilities is natural and part of who we are. One can become a personal communicator without hanging out a shingle. We must realize that discarnates are always seeking ways to communicate directly as they seek to let you know that they are still around. The direct reception of after death communication has always occurred, will continue to happen, and receiving a sign or message is not indicative that one has a special gift that needs to be shared professionally. On the other hand, if your communications with discarnate entities are consistent and strong, and you are up to the challenge and willing to do the work, follow your bliss.

Are People Born Mediums, Or Can It Be Taught?

M ediums and researchers that I have interviewed over the years have different opinions on this question. Qualified mediums will be the first to tell you that we all possess the ability to communicate with those in other realms. Researchers tell us that we all have psi abilities to varying degrees, but most of us exhibit mediocre results in psi testing. When conducting research, occasionally subjects show extraordinary abilities that are way beyond the norm. In other words, our inherent psychic and mediumistic abilities vary greatly within a wide spectrum.

At one time these abilities were thought of the same way that we now refer to as our five senses, but over time they have become somewhat dormant as the result of our religious, cultural, and educational influences. Such influences often foster preoccupation with material possessions and instant gratification, while intuitive abilities fade into the background. It is analogous to other skills that become rusty due to inactivity and lack of practice. Although we all have intuitive abilities to some degree, some have stronger abilities in this area than others. It is not unlike the differences between professional and recreational athletes. Many people are pretty good at hitting or catching a baseball, but few have the natural ability to make it to the big leagues, despite practice and dedication. However, some athletes have very strong innate ability and through dedicated training hone their skills and become professionals. Similarly, some can be recreational mediums with some intuitive ability, but they do not have what it takes to become a professional medium. However, some with raw but strong intuitive abilities take it further, attend mediumship development training classes, and some eventually become proficient professional mediums.

I would venture to say that the vast majority should be content with fostering their own gifts without seeking a career in mediumship. The bottom line is that, in my opinion, there must be some extremely strong intuitive ability before one should consider becoming a practicing medium. This ability can most definitely be honed and improved, but it is rare that someone becomes a medium from "scratch."

What Can I Do to Hone My Own Abilities?

Since intuitive abilities are inherent to our nature there is no reason why we should not be able to bring them to the forefront. In fact, it may be part of our purpose to recognize the abilities that we were designed to possess. I am not talking about becoming professional mediums but reaffirming our purpose as personal communicators to those who reside in realms that we rarely see. Recognition of an interconnected universe could very well result in a better existence in the physical and beyond.

The first step in the process is the most important, which is the simple belief that such communication is possible. It sounds obvious, but what could be a greater impediment than starting off with an emotional and intellectual block? Remaining open to being an antenna for information and setting your own conscious thoughts and interpretations aside is a good start. Practitioners stress meditation as a vehicle for accomplishing this state of mind. Through meditation one can reach an altered state of consciousness, which is essentially the state in which mediums work. Altered states can be achieved through other means as well, such as sensory deprivation, surrounding oneself in nature, psychoactive substances and through being immersed in music, art, or literature.

Many also find it helpful to set an intention by asking a deceased loved one, either vocally or through thought, to come visit in a dream. Since dreaming occurs in an altered state of consciousness, information seems to flow while in this condition. Perhaps the dream state provides a conduit that is recognized by those in the non-physical realm. It is as if they see an opening and take advantage of the conditions. Since mediumship is considered to be a telepathic process, engaging in psychic exercises may very well be an aid to spirit communication. There are many books on fostering dream visits and psychic exercises, some of which can be found in the recommended books section of this book.

ARE MEDIUM BRAINS DIFFERENT?

It is thought by some scientists that the brain plays a role in intuitive and psychic abilities. It is quite possible that certain areas of the brain may act as receptors of non-local information. It has also been conjectured that the brain acts as a filter for such information, and without the filter we would be bombarded by all sorts of communications that emanate from sources that have nothing to do with the physical senses. Much of materialist science believes that phenomena such as near-death experiences, dream visitations, deathbed visions, etc. are simply hallucinations generated by the brain. However, the evidence suggests that the brain is not the generator of the experience but allows us to receive and interpret information that emanates from non-physical sources. It is theorized that certain parts or substances in the brain may play a role in such reception. It is fact, as evidenced by phenomena such as telepathy, remote viewing, distant – healing, and other types of clairvoyance that our minds can act independently of our physical brains.

Scientific studies continue to be conducted with brain imaging to identify areas in the brain that exhibit changes during meditation or altered states of consciousness. Mediums fit into this category, as they are certainly in an altered state when communicating with spirit. It has been shown that the brains of mediums show different patterns of activity when they are engaged in spirit communication. Specific brain areas either light up or go dark for people in such states, suggesting that brain mapping could one day identify ways in which we could all generate or enhance our intuitive abilities.

It has been my observation over the years that evidential mediums seem to fit the classic description of being right-brained dominant. The overwhelming percentage of such mediums also exhibit associated abilities in such endeavors as music, art, writing, etc. In other words, people creative in the arts appear to be best suited for mediumship. Things usually associated with left-brained thinking, such as being logical, analytical, and objective, appear to inhibit the practice. I do not mean to suggest that mediums do not have the ability to be strong analytical thinkers – they are simply able to put that part of themselves aside when engaged in mediumship activity.

One last thought about the role of the brain in psi phenomena. I, as do some others, do not discount the possibility that the heart plays an essential role. As a matter of fact, we cannot say that the heart is less important to the subject of consciousness than the brain. Is it not possible that some information from non-local sources bypasses the brain and is received directly by the heart? Perhaps that might explain our pure subjective experiences that we simply experience without interpretation.

ARE MEDIUMS SPIRITUAL AND DO THEY DO SPIRITUAL WORK?

Having been involved in the corporate world for my entire adult life, the prospect of working with scientists who studied non-physical phenomena, mediums, metaphysical practitioners, etc. was welcomed with great anticipation. I would finally be amidst spiritual folks, much removed from the pressures, greed, and coldness of the business environment. However, was I surprised! Mediums, scientists, researchers, and medical doctors are just like the rest of us as they navigate their physical lives. I quickly learned that scientists and researchers are often understandably protective of their work as each competes for a piece of the meager number of grants available in the field. Medical doctors often must keep such research hidden from their peers for fear of ruining their careers. You may be thinking, "But mediums must be different, as anyone who can communicate with the dead surely must have a greater awareness of the value of compassion and love." Just like everyone else, some do, and some do not.

Should what mediums do be described as magical, mystical, supernormal, or spiritual? I think that it is fair to say that among the public all these descriptions are often heard. Some people believe that the process of talking to the dead falls under the heading of magic, as it is something that cannot happen according to common thought. So, if someone believes that it is impossible to occur, they put it in the category of trickery. Of course, this is faulty reasoning, as anyone with knowledge of science must admit that many of the concepts that we now take for granted were once scorned and ridiculed, or worse. Some of today's most esteemed scientists would have been considered magical thinkers not that long ago.

Those who describe spirit communication as something mystical most likely believe that discarnate communication is taking place, but such things are unexplainable, emanate from an unknown process or source, and perhaps should remain secret. Some associate such things with fear or danger, most likely the result of media conditioning or religious orientation. Of course, the mystery schools of thought were based on visionary experiences, pre-dated organized religion and dominated our heritage for thousands of years.

That brings us to the supernormal classification, which certainly seems accurate as mediumship takes place not through our known physical senses, but by non-physical means, therefore being beyond normal. However, who is to say that these senses that we deem to be beyond the capabilities of mortal beings are not inherent to us all – thus making them normal? It is quite possible that these abilities were evident among the masses in ancient times, and ever since have waned and atrophied due to non-use. Certainly, the age of instant communication and information is not conducive to telepathic development and inner exploration.

When we discuss mediums and spirituality it gets tricky. In fact, many mediums today bill themselves as spiritual mediums. Is spirit communication a spiritual endeavor or have nothing to do with spirituality? Is it simply an ability that one possesses to communicate with people who are no longer in physical form? It depends on how one defines spirituality. If you believe that the process is sacred, part of higher knowledge and design, and something to be treated with awe and respect, then calling it a spiritual practice seems fair and accurate. This form of spirituality is not to be confused with organized religions that often have rules that must be obeyed and may shun and disparage the flock from participating in forbidden practices.

However, over the years I have encountered some mediums that appear to be the antithesis of spiritual beings. These folks do not work for the greater good, show little compassion and empathy, and do not portray mediumship with the respect it demands and deserves. Yet, these same mediums are sometimes very proficient in evidential mediumship over long careers. In view of this, I can certainly make the argument that, at least among this group, mediumship ability has nothing to do with spirituality.

We all can provide examples of telepathy, mind to mind communication, that occur in our daily lives. From a scientific standpoint, the evidence is incontrovertible that this phenomenon is real and inherent to us all in varying degrees. I have heard very few people describe psychic ability as being spiritual in nature. If we think of mediumship as a telepathic process, the only difference being that one of the participants no longer has a physical body, it seems illogical to assume that the communication is spiritual in nature. Our loved ones in spirit want to remain part of our lives, need to get messages through to us when they are unable to reach us directly, and gifted mediums are the conduits by which the connection is made. We know that radios receive signals that are invisible to us, but would you call a radio spiritual? It may sound like a clinical description to some who would prefer an unworldly explanation, but perhaps we read more into such things than is necessary. This is not to underestimate the valuable service that excellent mediums provide – quite the contrary. I constantly see mediums change the lives of the people who sit before them. Describing them as lifelines may be more accurate than conduits. In that sense, the work that they do should be considered spiritual, as who can say that the universe does not have a hand in the connection?

We call the afterlife a spirit realm to differentiate it from the physical realm. Many believe that those in the spirit realm will refuse to communicate through mediums with whom they do not resonate. Those free of the physical body may be better able to discern the motives and compassion of the medium. This could explain why communication sometimes does not take place in a sitting and why some mediums find that their abilities wane later in their careers, especially among those who have succumbed to the ego mind of the physical world.

Do Mediums Grieve, and Do They Feel Physical Effects?

T his is something that I initially pondered, and we often get asked. I used to think that mediums had a distinct advantage over the rest of us who grieve the loss of a loved one. After all, from their perspective of communicating with the dead virtually every day, their loved ones are only in the next room. However, I came to realize that mediums grieve the same way as everyone else. Human emotions take precedence over intellectual reasoning, knowledge, and experience, and despite knowing that loved ones still exist the pain of missing them in the physical is real. Also, most mediums tell us that they are rarely able to connect with their own deceased loved ones. Apparently, the emotions affect the process, and mediums wishing to connect to their own loved ones usually seek out the services of other mediums. However, mediums are like the general population in one respect, as their experiential knowledge and awareness of afterlife research have positive effects on their grief.

I sometimes get a bit anxious in group readings if the medium starts talking about their own grief over a deceased loved one. I imagine the attendees thinking that if the medium shows grief, knowing what they know, their road to healing is going to be rough. However, mediums are people too and are certainly entitled to grieve in their own ways like the rest of us. I would just caution them to always keep in mind the fragile state of the attendees.

It is sometimes said that mediums suffer adverse physical effects to their health due to their work. Although there are few scientific studies that researched this question, I have read that many of the trance and physical mediums in history developed illnesses and conditions that they attributed to their work. I have also noticed that a large percentage of today's mental mediums do have various physical problems, but more studies and statistical analyses would need to be done to determine if this is significantly different from the general population. It is possible that the constant flow of thought and energy, both positive and negative, could have a harmful physical effect on the medium. I have observed mediums at the end of long sessions, and many appear physically drained and exhausted. If the theory is true that a medium must raise their vibratory level to conduct spirit communication, sustaining such a state for a long period of time must be taxing. In addition, since mediums are empathic by nature, and keeping in mind that discarnates usually convey to the medium the way in which they died, absorbing this information may take a physical and mental toll on the medium.

Another observation is that it appears that a very large percentage of practicing mediums have suffered either physical or emotional trauma in their childhood. Whether or not this acted as some sort of trigger for their intuitive abilities is unknown, but it would certainly make for an interesting study. Perhaps such trauma, which often is accompanied by disassociation as the medium escapes to other "realms", somehow better prepared them for mediumship as they were already accomplished in putting their rational mind aside. We already know that the trauma of a near death experience often results in heightened intuitive ability, so these connections need to be explored in depth.

THE PUBLIC PERCEPTION
OF MEDIUMS

Not long ago I sent out some emails soliciting quotes from companies that offer grant assistance to not for profit foundations. In the emails I explained the scope of the foundation and specifically where we needed assistance. One response was from a company representative who said that not only would he not provide a quote, but he would never be involved with an organization that preys on the bereaved. His exact response was: "I absolutely would not help an organization that promotes frauds such as mediums and psychics. Those people leech off the bereaved and offer false hope to the grieving. I only work with rational, evidence-based nonprofits doing social good."

Certainly, this was not the first time that we have encountered ignorant skeptics, as we have been trying to educate the uninformed for seventeen years and are well-aware of public perception. My response to this individual began with my usual suggestion that he become aware of the established evidence about non-physical phenomena and continued with a brief overview of the history of mediumship research from credible scientists. However, as I continued writing I found that my usual balanced response was being taken over by raw emotion. I ended my email by stating that, as a well-informed bereaved parent, I would like to get on a plane to visit him (in England) for the sole purpose of punching him in the face .... but he wasn't worth my time. I am not proud of my response, especially recognizing that I was once him. I was totally ignorant of the established evidence and not willing to contemplate concepts that made little sense to my way of thinking. Emotional trauma triggered my exploration and transformation, but how might others become interested enough to learn about such things? The fact is, there are far more people in the world like my correspondent than there are those who are aware of the nature of mediumship. The prevailing view about mediums is one of scorn, mockery, disbelief, and anger. Even worse, the researchers that study mediumship and related phenomena face similar disdain from their peers in the scientific community.

However, as evidenced by history, we know that many initially ridiculed for their research and discoveries were later heralded as pioneers in science. Change is a slow process, as is education. The best route to changing worldview about something is to remain steadfast in providing reliable information. Human nature is such that many need the assurance that others feel the same way as they do before accepting new beliefs. The herd mentality is very strong and often dangerous. So, the evidence is out there, but even more important are the personal experiences that so many keep hidden.

My humble advice to those who are interested in effecting change in the way we view death is to share what they have learned and what they have experienced.

CAN I SCORE A READING TO
DETERMINE IF IT WAS EVIDENTIAL?

There is an efficient and simple way of scoring a medium reading to determine if the information you received was evidential. The scoring process that Forever Family Foundation uses in their medium evaluation certification sessions is comprehensive, but the following short method should prove to be useful and accurate. To score the reading effectively you will need to either take notes during the reading or record the session for later reference. Scoring the reading from a recording is the preferred method, as you can make the notes with no time pressures and be sure of what was said.

All you will need is a pad of paper and pen. As you play back the recording of the session, make a notation for each piece of information given to you by the medium. This is not meant to be a transcription of the session, but general notes. In other words, let us say the medium said, "I have your grandmother here and I sense that she was a heavy smoker." On your pad you might write "grandmother-smoker." Follow this procedure and make notes line by line for each new piece of information.

On the right side of your piece of paper, make four small columns and label them: "significant hit", "hit", "miss" and "maybe". You will be checking the applicable box next to each piece of information. A "hit" is a piece of information that you know to be true. For example, if the medium said that she has your mom in spirit, and your mom is passed, that would be a true statement and marked as a "hit." A "miss" is a piece of information that you know not to be true. If the medium said she had your mom in spirit, and your mom was very much alive, that statement would be marked as a "miss." A "maybe" is a statement that you cannot verify to be true or false. So if the medium said that you had a great uncle who worked for the post office, and you never knew any of your great uncles, you would mark this statement as a "maybe." Of course, you may wish to later change the scoring of "maybes", as you may discover that the statement was either a clear "hit" or a "miss". That leaves us with one category yet unexplained, the "significant hit". This is a "hit" that is not only true, but extremely specific. For example, if the medium says, "I have your father in spirit", you will mark that as a "hit" if your father is deceased. However, if the medium said, "I have your deceased father Irving here," and your father's name was Irving, that becomes a "significant hit". This designation becomes important to the scoring as we want to give a piece of information that is very specific or obscure more weight than a general statement that may be true. Please note that you are scoring such a statement as a "significant hit" only (not in addition to a "hit".)

When you are done evaluating each piece of information given to you by the medium, add up the total number of statements (no matter how you scored them) and write down that number. The total number of statements includes "significant hits", "hits", "misses" and "maybes". The next step is to look at your columns and add the total number of "hits" and "significant hits." Each "hit" has a point value of 1, and each "significant hit" has a point value of 2. Divide the total number of "hits" by the total pieces of information given to you by the medium. In other words, if the total point value of hits were 10, and there was a total of 25 pieces of information given, you would calculate 10 divided by 25, which equals 40%.

After calculating the percentage of hits, if it exceeds 60% it is indicative of an evidential reading. Bear in mind that the average reading will contain many "maybes," which we are counting in the total pieces of information. If we were not to count the "maybes" in our scoring the percentages needed for an evidential reading would be much higher, and in the 85% range.

Description of Forever Family Foundation's Medium Certification Evaluation Process

Forever Family Foundation's process is not a scientific endeavor nor is it a research project. Although it is conducted under controlled conditions and based upon some elements of scientific design, it lacks the blinded protocol that is a necessary component of scientific research. Instead, the foundation evaluates the evidence under conditions in which the medium usually works while sitting with a client.

The foundation website and literature list an email address for those mediums wishing to apply for certification. The website goes into detail about the process, including what type of candidate should apply. The foundation never solicits or seeks out mediums, and the program is conducted free of charge. Similarly, once certified, mediums do not pay to be listed on the website resource page.

The first step requires the medium to send an email that expresses their wish to apply for participation in the process. Upon receipt of such an email, a reply is sent with a request that the medium answer some basic questions about their ability and reasons for seeking certification, including one question that shows their familiarity with the work of Forever Family Foundation. Assuming that the answers are acceptable to the Medium Evaluation Committee, the medium is then sent a complete description of the process and invited to complete an extensive on-line application.

Upon receipt of a completed application it is reviewed by committee to determine if the evaluation process should continue. There are certain red flags that are looked for regarding ethics, experience, ability, and reasons for wanting to be certified. If the committee determines that the applicant qualifies to continue in the process, a telephone interview is a arranged. The interview is comprehensive by design, and the interviewer then provides a numerical score based upon their interview evaluation. The interview and application are reviewed and a decision whether to invite the medium to participate in a future evaluation session is made.

The sessions themselves take place via the internet using meeting software, which means that mediums can participate regardless of where in the world they reside. Since webcams are used, the medium and the sitter can see each other, just as they would during a personal reading with a client. The foundation maintains a pool of trained sitters to be part of the process. Each sitter is a foundation member and well versed in the scoring process, and steps are taken to ensure that the sitter has no prior knowledge of any of the participating mediums. During the readings, the sitters are aware that they cannot divulge information to the mediums, but it is important that they respond with "yes" or "no" type answers to the mediums.

Each medium is required to do a total of five readings, each fifteen minutes in duration, and each with a different sitter. One of the readings is done without video, so the medium and sitter are not able to see each other. The other four readings are done with video, with each medium and sitter placed in a private dedicated breakout room. Each medium will read for a total of five different trained sitters. At the end of each reading the sitter scores the evidence that has been received. Sitters can also refer to their notes to continue or amend their scoring. Scoring sheets are submitted after the sitter is confident with their scores, and after their further investigation into information that could not be verified during the process.

Five different statistical scoring methods are used as the composite results are tabulated. To gain certification the medium must meet the minimum guidelines in each of the scoring methods, and the proficiency bar is set high.

Only a small percentage of the applicants invited to complete an application follow through with the submission. I suspect that many mediums think that this is a simple process that involves paying a fee, possibly doing a simple reading for an administrator, then receiving a seal of approval that they could put on their website to increase their business. However, once they recognize that only highly developed mediums have a chance of passing, the application is never completed.

If a medium fails to gain the foundation's certification does that mean that they are not a capable medium? No, it only means that during the process, under controlled conditions, they failed to meet the foundation's standards. There could be several explanations, only one of which is a true reflection of their ability. We know that mediums are not used to being evaluated under somewhat clinical conditions. The process itself might throw them off their game, or the technology used could interfere with their communications with spirit. For this reason, mediums are permitted to participate in a future session should they wish to try the process again.

The foundation's experience is that mediums who have gained its certification have been consistent in producing evidence, and many have gone on to successfully participate in scientific research. The process is not a perfect system by any means; however, it has proven to be an effective way of identifying mediums who demonstrate high proficiency without the use of deception or fraud. Most importantly it has been an effective resource tool in protecting the bereaved.

Personal Experiences Backed Up by Science

The following accounts are all true and are personal experiences that I continuously chalked up to coincidence. That is until I eventually relented over the preponderance of evidence. These represent my personal proof of survival, and combined with knowledge of the scientific evidence, have formed a powerful base upon which I have been able to create a meaningful and purposeful life. We have heard countless numbers of similar accounts from foundation membership over the years, and these are only some personal examples. After Death encounters occur on a regular basis and have little to do with one's culture, religious beliefs, and education. These communications are often missed or disregarded by those wearing materialist blinders, but they occur, nonetheless.

The Blue Magic Marker

After my daughter Bailey's funeral, my wife Phran was visited by Bailey's best friend Ally. Ally related the fact that, several years earlier when they were both twelve years old, Bailey convinced her to enter a pact between the two. Bailey outlined the terms of the pact, which were that they were each to make up a sign that they would communicate to the other in the event of either of their deaths. Bailey's sign was that she was going to place a blue "magic marker" in a place that it would ordinarily not be found. Ally described to Phran that when she returned home after Bailey's funeral and entered her room, neatly placed on her computer keyboard was a blue "magic marker." What made this especially significant was the fact that Ally did not own such a marker, and certainly was not using one. Ally checked with other family members to see if they had been in her room, and they were not.

Science continues to identify the existence of psychokinesis, the ability of mind to affect matter. If our consciousness does survive physical death, there is reason to assume that discarnates can play a role in this phenomenon the same way as those with a body. Movement of objects and energy manipulations such as lights going on and off are commonly reported in after death communications.

The Room Visit

When Bailey was nine years old our family moved to a new home, and she was not happy about leaving her friends, her school, and the room in the home she adored. She eventually settled into her new surroundings but, even as the years passed by, she would continuously try to convince Phran to drive her to our old home so that she could request seeing her old room once more. Phran would always explain that we did not know the new residents of the old home and such an action would not be appropriate.

As it turned out, Phran's cousin did know the people that bought our old home. Not long after Bailey's death Phran's cousin was at an event that was also attended by these people. The homeowner approached Phran's cousin to express her condolences about Bailey's death and asked if she could share something that had happened. It turns out that the woman's daughter had chosen the same room in the home that was Bailey's as an infant and young child. One evening the woman's daughter described the experience of seeing a young girl walking around her room and was somewhat agitated by the experience. Her mother, chalking it up to a bad dream, reassured her daughter that it was not real, and her daughter returned to her room to sleep.

The next morning, as the mother was having a cup of coffee, she placed the morning newspaper on the table and was startled by the story on the front page that described Bailey's accident and subsequent death. She recognized our name and knew we were the people from whom she purchased the house. As she read further, she realized that her daughter's vision occurred very shortly after Bailey's death.

Apparitions and ghosts have been described and written about for thousands of years. They are obviously hard to research under laboratory conditions as they are spontaneous occurrences, but they happen all the time, nonetheless. As I reflected upon the circumstances described above, what made this event particularly compelling were the facts leading up to it. Bailey always seemed to be compelled to visit her old room, and never let go. Once freed of the physical body and recognizing the fact that by thought alone she could transport herself to wherever she wished to go, seeing her old room would certainly be on top of her list. I was appreciative of this confirmation, and although I was still in denial about survival, it certainly provided a glimmer of hope.

The Morse Code

About a year after Bailey's death we bought a new car for Phran. One day she described driving in the car and hearing what she could only describe as Morse Code coming out of the radio, even though the radio was turned off at the time. It was a very specific cadence of rapid sounds, which is why the code came to mind. When she explained this to me, I assured her that electronic bugs were very common in new cars, and I would have it checked out when we brought it in for the first service.

A few weeks later I was driving her car, listening to the radio, when I heard the same cadence. I immediately turned the radio off, but the code continued. OK, now it had my attention. A couple of weeks after that Phran was driving my car and heard the same cadence that she heard in her car. Phran then decided to conduct her own experiment by bringing a tape recorder with her on a trip in her new car. As she started the car, she turned on the tape recorder, but realized that she had left something she needed in the house and left the car to retrieve the item. When she later played back the tape, she heard the cadence that was recorded at the same time she was out of the car.

Shortly thereafter I was driving my car to work, a car I had been driving for more than two years, and the cadence started coming out of my radio, both on and off. This obviously intrigued me even more. In the ensuing months, the same code started coming out of every electrical apparatus that we owned. Televisions emitted the code whether on or off, as did computers, alarm panels, and appliances that had no speakers. During this same time, we were visited by Dr. Gary Schwartz who was in town to present at a large afterlife lecture that the foundation was hosting at a local university. In the middle of the lecture, as Gary was speaking, the same cadence started coming out of the auditorium speakers. Since Gary already knew about the phenomenon, he stopped his talk for a few seconds to spot me in the audience with a look of wonderment.

After hearing more about our descriptions about the Morse Code phenomenon, Gary suggested that we conduct an experiment to determine if, in fact, Bailey was sending this code. He asked Phran to talk to Bailey and ask her if it were she that was sending us these codes, and if so, she should communicate with a research medium named Janet Mayer to let Janet know. Gary was involved with Janet in a mediumship research project and they communicated with each other regularly. Neither Phran nor I knew who Janet was and we had never met or spoken to her.

Phran followed directions, lit a candle, and sent a request to Bailey. She asked Bailey to please visit this medium who was unknown to us, but who resided in St. Louis, Missouri. She also asked Bailey to be very specific and be sure to mention the words "Morse Code."

The next day I went to my office and turned on my computer to check my emails. The first email I opened was from Gary and it was a forward of an email that he received that morning from Janet. In the body of the email Janet said "Gary, I have no idea what this means, I have never experienced anything like this before, but someone is sending me Morse Code."

I remember voicing an audible gasp, evidently loud enough for someone else in the office to come ask me what was happened. What I had just read was mind-blowing and a real challenge to my logic and sensibility. How was this possible? How does someone not in the physical hone – in on a specific medium and relay the exact words that were requested? I knew that there was no collusion or communication between Gary and Janet about this impromptu experiment, and certainly neither Phran nor I spoke to Janet.

Some would say that, as incredible as this communication was, it does not represent proof of survival. It could be the result of "super-psi," which theorizes a vast storehouse of information from which one can identify and extract specifics. To me, that explanation seems less plausible than the survival hypothesis. Furthermore, survival of consciousness and the super-psi theory are not mutually exclusive, and both could be in play during such experiences. Whichever explanation you choose to believe, one thing is clear, it defies materialist thinking that consciousness is generated by and confined to our physical body.

The Dream Visits

My middle child, Kori, returned to her freshman year of college at Carnegie Mellon University a week after Bailey's funeral. This is what she wanted to do, and we all agreed that everyone must follow their own instincts when grieving. About a month later we decided to take a flight to Pittsburgh for parents' weekend to visit with Kori and make sure that she was coping the best that she could. Phran, I, my son Jonathan and his girlfriend at the time traveled together. We all stayed in the same hotel, and Kori decided to stay in the hotel as well.

Jonathan had made a miraculous recovery from his injuries and was well enough to make the trip. We had dinner in a local restaurant, and we all retired to our hotel rooms for the evening. Up until this point, despite that only a short time had passed since Bailey's death, Phran was fortunate enough to have had many personal experiences that involved after death communications. Although I was quite jealous and yearned for my own experience, Phran's occurrences were something of a lifeline to me as I struggled to keep my sanity. I knew that Phran would never lie to me about anything, and these experiences gave me a glimmer of hope.

During the night Bailey came to me in a dream, and we were able to talk and hug. I woke up with my heart pounding out of my chest, to the point that Phran was ready to drive me to an emergency room for fear that I was having a heart attack. The experience was so vivid and real that my emotions were out of control as I tried to assimilate what had just happened. I eventually calmed down and was able to return to sleep, only to experience two more visits from Bailey. When I awoke in the morning, I learned from Phran that she also had a visit from Bailey during the night. Later, when we all met for breakfast, I was amazed to find out that both Kori and Jonathan's girlfriend also had Bailey visits during the night!

Four separate people, three of whom had never had such a visit or even knew that it was possible, all had individual visits during the same time in the same location. I could not fail to see the significance, and it sure seemed as if Bailey were providing a giant hello and confirmation that she still survived.

Such visits from discarnates during the dream state are quite common, and the theory is that those in spirit have an easier time communicating with us when our filters are at rest and we are better able to receive. There is also the question of how an entity could appear to four different people at the same time. Those in other realms are not tethered by the physical laws that dictate life in the physical world. Or some would say that this is the dream world and when we dream, we visit the real world. When we dream, we enter consciousness that has no boundaries, and space/time is not linear to those in the spirit world. Some who have near death experiences describe being out of their bodies and able to be at many locations simultaneously. It is a hard concept to grasp using our current understanding. That is why those who catch glimpses of the next life tell us that the experience is ineffable, simply impossible to put into words.

Getting a Message Across

After the accident, my son Jonathan slowly started to recover from his brain injuries and was eventually released from the hospital to enter an out-patient facility. Phran and I worked out our schedule so that I would drop him off at the facility in the morning and Phran would pick him up at the end of the day. One late afternoon, while on the way to get Jonathan, Phran was overcome by thoughts of a nine-year old child who was killed eleven years earlier in a freak accident at school. The child, Bryanna West (name changed) was crushed by closing automatic gym doors. Phran, as PTA President, happened to be at the school that day. Not only was she thinking of Bryanna, but she was consumed with finding out how old she would now be. Phran was so overwhelmed that she had to pull the car off the road while she attempted to compose herself. After calming down, she continued her journey to pick up Jonathan.

Meanwhile, our grief was becoming more than we could handle and I desperately sought out a support group that we could attend. I finally located one that was meeting that night. I was already home when Phran arrived and I announced that we needed to leave immediately to make the hour drive to this meeting. During the drive Phran filled me in on the experience she had earlier. We arrived at the meeting in time and we were seated in the front row of seats. Much to my discomfort, the meeting started with each parent asked to announce who they were, the name of the child that they lost, and a little description of why they were there. We were waiting our turn to speak when a woman said, "My name is Kathy West," at which time I felt Phran's fingernails dig into my skin. The woman continued, "Mother of Bryanna West."

After the meeting Phran re-introduced herself to Kathy and simply said "I just want to let you know that I was thinking of Bryanna today." Kathy looked at Phran and replied, "Oh, how nice, today is Bryanna's 21st birthday."

In thinking about this later, my first reaction was to chalk yet another experience up to coincidence. However, when I examined the facts, something else seemed to be at play. Looking at it objectively I realized that here we had a mother (Phran) who was completely devastated by the recent loss of her own daughter (Bailey), yet became completely overwhelmed by the thought of another child that she had not thought about for over a decade. Furthermore, she was consumed with finding out this child's age, which is unusual in and of itself. We later travel to a meeting at the spur of a moment, and the child's parents are there, and it is the child's 21st birthday. The most plausible explanation is that Bryanna, in spirit, needed to get a message through to her mother, most likely because she was unable to do this directly. Bryanna, seeing a bigger picture, knew that Phran would be seeing her mother that evening, and knew that Phran would get the message across.

The implication is that those is spirit not only keep track of what is going on in our lives but are quite inventive in ways that they can connect. My interpretation is that, in this case, Bryanna conveyed thoughts and emotions to Phran, who was evidently a good conduit. The literature is filled with similar accounts of those in spirit communicating through third parties.

Another Inventive Message

I have had over seventy visits from my daughter Bailey while I was in the dream state, and I have journaled each one. For some reason, I sometimes have visits from deceased persons that I knew casually in the physical, or never knew. I will readily admit that, regarding intuitive abilities, I am useless in the conscious state but apparently somewhat useful while unconscious.

We have friends, Joe and Maryann, who are active volunteers of Forever Family Foundation. We met them after the passing of their daughter Jessica, and I never had the honor of meeting Jessica, nor had I been to Joe and Maryanne's home. One night while dreaming I was visited by a young lady who I instantly recognized as being Jessica. I cannot explain how I knew, as I never saw a photo of her, but I instinctively knew it was her. She and I had a nice conversation and visit in her home while she was standing in front of a wall of windows, and she told me the story of how she and her dad built the pool in the backyard with the stone border. Due to the research that I had already done, during this dream visit I knew to try to keep lucid and track of as much detail as possible, for evidentiary purposes.

After this visit I knew that I had to contact her parents. This would ordinarily be a delicate task but knowing her parents I knew that they would be open to such information. I called them and tried to be as evidential as possible, trying to recall every detail. I told them Jessica's height, eye color, hair color, and the way she wore her hair. I described the wall of glass overlooking a huge backyard and the pool she built with Joe. As it turned out, everything matched except for the pool. Jessica and her dad built a pond, with the stone border, but I interpreted it as a pool.

As it turned out, Maryann had been struggling with trying to achieve a personal connection to Jessica, who evidently found me to be a suitable messenger. I was honored to meet her and to deliver the healing message to the people she loved the most. My heart was especially warmed when, about six months later, I saw Joe and Maryann and they showed me a photograph of Jessica. It was the same exact girl that paid me a visit.

It is important to note that all of us have these abilities, even a doubting left brained non-intuitive person such as me. It is a mistake to believe that only mediums can communicate with the dead, and mediums will be the first to confirm this fact. By the way, it would have been a big mistake on my part to interpret this incident as an indication that I was meant to be a medium. I simply took it for what it was, someone in spirit using me to get a message across, something that happens to us all more often than you think.

Super Bowl

For many years we held an annual Super Bowl party in our home, hosted by our son Jonathan. During one such Jonathan invited the parents of a couple whose son was a student of Jonathan's in a karate school. The woman got into a discussion with Phran and happened to mention that they live in an old historic home. Phran could not resist, and asked "Might there be any spirits in your home?" Never knowing how people will react to such a question, Phran was pleased to hear "Well, as a matter of fact, yes there are!"

The woman then proceeded to tell Phran that her home was two hundred years old and was built with a nursery attached to the master bedroom. When her first child was born and placed in the nursery, the child would always cry and refuse to sleep. It happened every single time they attempted to put the child to sleep in the nursery, and they eventually stopped trying and moved the child to another bedroom where he slept beautifully. When their second child was born, once again they put the child in the nursery, but experienced the same results. This child was also moved to another bedroom where he flourished. The children got older and the parents decided that they no longer needed a nursery, had the walls knocked down and expanded the master bedroom.

Shortly after the nursery was eliminated all sorts of unexplained phenomena started happening in the home. Windows that were sealed shut for a century started opening and closing by themselves. Drawers and closet doors would open and close, objects would move, and various unexplained sounds and footsteps were heard. The woman researched mediums and had one come to her home. The medium proceeded to tell her that the house was inhabited by a woman dressed in black whose baby had died in the nursery. The deceased woman stayed mainly in the nursery and was accompanied by a man who sat in a rocking chair smoking a pipe. Prior to the medium's visit to the home, the children of the present owner often told their mother that they occasionally saw a woman dressed in black walking in the home.

The woman was relaying this information while thirty people were watching the big game in our den. As soon as the woman told Phran about the various phenomena that occurred in her home, the electric power in our home blacked out. As you might imagine, the people watching the game were not pleased. There was no apparent reason for the loss of power. The weather was perfect, with no wind, rain or other adverse conditions that might cause an interruption. No circuit breakers were tripped, and no neighbors lost power. The outage lasted a few minutes only and game watching resumed. Phran's comment was "I guess you brought a few of the spirits with you." During the rest of the game, as the woman continued to discuss her house phenomena, a subsequent blackout again occurred in my home. The natives were getting restless, but the good food and drink placated some of the guests until power resumed.

The couple that had house spirits left during halftime of the game, and Phran and I were sitting on the couch with Chris, a friend of Jonathan, and Richard, an old college buddy of mine. Chris had evidently heard some of the house phenomena story and asked Phran if she "believed in all this stuff." Phran began by stating that much of the phenomena are indeed real but exaggerated by the media. Chris asked if Phran had seen the movie "White Noise," and added that most of those movies are scary. Richard asked Phran to explain what was meant by white noise, and Phran asked if he ever saw a TV that was turned to a non-broadcasting station. As if on cue, as soon as she uttered these words, our TV went to a non – broadcasting station and the screen showed only the static noise and patterns. With that, Chris jumped up and said, "I'm out of here!" Richie, with a perplexed look on his face, took out his checkbook and made a donation to Forever Family Foundation.

Electronic Voice Phenomena and Instrumental Transcommunication continue to be reported in great numbers and researched by organizations such as ATransC (atransc.org). Spirit entities are sometimes able to carve images out of a static type background and produce voices on recording tape. Our Super Bowl experience was not specifically illustrative of these phenomena, but certainly illustrated how discarnates can manipulate energy. This also appears to show that some discarnate entities do have attachments to the physical world, at least until they move on.

Evidential Mediumship

In my darkest days soon after the passing of my daughter, Phran & I went to visit a well-known medium. Although logic told me that communication with the dead was preposterous, I was open to anything that had a chance of providing any respite from my grief. This was a group reading with approximately 10-12 people in attendance and was held in a hotel room. I sat there in the dimly lit room wondering how the hell I wound up there, as the setting seemed somewhat absurd.

I will address each of the three evidential statements given to me by first providing some background for each. I relate these as an example of truly evidential mediumship:

1) Ever since she was a toddler my daughter would constantly try to get me to admit that she was my favorite. She was relentless through the years, saying, "C'mon dad, admit it, you know I am your favorite." It was our little joke. I would always respond that I love all my children equally and would never say that. Soon after Bailey died, I went to visit her grave and said "OK, I admit it – you were my favorite"

During the session, the medium addressed me and said "Dad, your daughter wants me to tell you that she knows that she was your favorite!"

OK – the medium now had my attention

2) A few days before going to the medium session Phran was sleeping and awoke to an inner suggestion that our home was filling up with smoke. Immediately upon awakening, she smelled smoke in the house, and started to investigate. She walked through all three floors of our home, continuing to smell smoke, but found nothing that might cause smoke to be emitted.

The medium next said to me "Dad, your daughter is telling me that you will know when she is around by the smell of smoke!"

Hmmm – this was now getting a bit crazy.

3) Soon after Bailey's passing Phran and my daughter Kori went on Bailey's computer and discovered a treasure trove of poems, short stories, and essays that she had written but never shared. We compiled these writings and published them in a book entitled *Hidden Treasures*.

The medium next said to me, "By the way, she is telling me that she is happy that you found all of her writings!"

I do not remember the drive home that night as my mind was racing with a myriad of thoughts and emotions. One side of me told me that the information had to be coincidence; the other side provided the first ray of hope in my grief as I was excited by the prospect that my daughter might possibly not only still exist, but be able to communicate.

Preventing a Heart Attack?

Shortly after the passing of Phran's mom we took a short vacation in Sedona, Arizona. The stress of my mother-in-law's extended illness and subsequent death left us emotionally and physically drained and we looked forward to some peaceful surroundings. The first night there I had a very clear dream visit from my mother-in-law, Barbara. We had a nice chat, and it was as if she never left. I told Phran about the visit in the morning, who was a bit jealous but happy that I heard from mom.

The second night featured yet another dream visitation from Barbara, which once again included pleasant conversation and a loving presence. When I told Phran the next morning, we both expressed surprise that Barbara was able to communicate less than a week after her physical death, and that I was able to receive the information.

The third night featured another visit, but this time it was not from Barbara. The visit was from Phran's deceased father Zoli who had passed in 1981. I adored Zoli while he was alive but had never received any signs or communications from him, and certainly was not thinking of him lately. In the visit he appeared before me with a serious look on his face and said in no uncertain terms "Bob, I need you to check something out – you have a blockage on the right side of your heart."

I guess that the message content and the clarity in which it was delivered shocked me a bit, as the visit ended abruptly and I woke up. I discussed this visit with Phran immediately, and I remember saying to her something like "shit, what the hell am I going to do with this information?" I went on to describe a scenario where I would go back to New York and set up an appointment with a cardiologist. When he asked me why I was there I would tell him that "my dead father-in-law told me that I had a heart blockage," and I would then watch the doctor's expression as he sized me up as a lunatic.

Phran remembered that we had gone to a spiritual medical doctor in Manhattan who also happened to be a Kabbalist. We thought that he would be the one doctor who would listen to the experience and not sit in judgment. I set up the appointment, told him about the dream visit message, and waited for his reaction. To my surprise he said, "I don't know about you, but I think it would be wise to heed the message and check this out." As it turned out I had several major risk factors that, left unchecked, surely would have resulted in a heart blockage. I was able to correct these issues through diet, supplements and life changes and no blockage or heart problems ensued. After my final visit to the doctor he looked at me and said, "I could work with your father-in-law!"

Dream visits are a commonly reported form of after death communication. Our loved ones in spirit apparently appreciate the opportunity to reach us while we are in an altered state of consciousness. Such visits can occur very soon after physical death, or decades later. Whether it has to do with a learned ability among those in spirit, a frequency match, or a shared resonance, it is important to remain open to the possibility and recognize the encounter when it occurs.

The Necklace

Not long after Bailey's passing we decided to see a medium that came highly recommended. Not knowing anything much about the mediumship process, Phran decided to put Bailey's necklace in her pocket to have with her at the reading. She did not show the necklace to the medium during the session. We were both extremely disappointed after the reading, as we did not hear one single piece of evidential information during the entire hour.

Phran and I left the medium's office and went our separate ways, as I went to work and Phran to run a bunch of errands. After completing the errands Phran returned home as she had an appointment for a friend to visit. As she started to unpack her shopping bags and place the necklace back in its rightful place, panic set in when she realized that the necklace was no longer in her pocket. She searched everywhere and then proceeded to call every store she had just visited to ask if they had found a necklace. None reported that a necklace was found. Phran's friend Debbie soon arrived and Phran went to let her in the front door. It was snowing out, and Debbie immediately sat down on the hallway bench so that she could remove her snowy boots.

They talked a while by the bench, Phran expressing her dismay at losing the necklace, and then both proceeded to the main part of the house. At the end of Debbie's visit the process was reversed as she sat down on the bench to put her boots back on. It was then that they both looked down at the floor in front of them, the same spot and floor where they had been conversing earlier and were amazed at what they saw. There it was, neatly placed in a circle as if it were on display, was the necklace.

I must admit that when I first heard this story I immediately started to think of material explanations, and questioned the possibility that the necklace could have fallen out of Phran's pocket, despite the fact that she searched the pocket many times. However, I soon realized that if you took a necklace and dropped it on the floor a million times, the likelihood is that it would never fall in a perfect circle as if it were placed. I found it more likely that my daughter was making up for our disappointing reading by letting us know that she continues to find ways to communicate directly.

The Wonder Awaits

A memorial service for my daughter was held at her high school shortly after her passing. Bailey's goal was to become an English teacher and she forged some strong relationships with her high school English teachers. The morning of the service day, her favorite teacher John went to clean out his storage cabinet in the teacher's lounge in preparation for the new school year that had not yet begun. Upon opening the cabinet doors, a lone computer disk fell onto the floor. John picked up the disk, which was unmarked, and he had never seen before, and was curious to see if it was blank or had content. He inserted the disk into the nearest computer. The disk contained a poem written by Bailey entitled "The Wonder Awaits," which appears below:

> I lay down to sleep
> on this one last evening
> wondering how much more
> until I'll be leaving
>
> And I think about
> the time that has past
> and I can't help believing
> that it might not last
>
> Is there an end
> and what after that
> do I go on
> or just disappear in a snap

The newspaper reads
of someone's death
and I wonder the chances
that I could be next

There are so many
horrible ways to die
I hope I go peacefully
with not a cry

My dreams of this moment
are a mist in the air
for of the dreams
I do not care

I await the moment
that I see the truth
do I live on
or in a silent booth

Each day I'm afraid
of the events to come
But maybe I shouldn't be
maybe death's not a bum

Maybe I'll like it
and maybe it's better
but that I will see
when G-d sends me that letter

The letter that says
it is time to go
the moment I feared
will finally show

And I will Go forth
to see what's in store
if I live on
or the rest is a bore

I only wish that
I could come back
to tell the world
of what death is in fact

The timing and circumstances of this occurrence are certainly compelling. The facts were not lost on me that the disk appeared out of nowhere, the day of her memorial, in a place that she loved and to a teacher that she adored. Did she manipulate the circumstances to make this poem appear when it did? Why did she not show it to anyone, including her teacher, until after her death? History is rich with after death communication accounts that involve psychokinesis, mind affecting matter. In addition, it certainly appears that some people, including many children, catch glimpses of their impending death. This poem, and many other poems, stories and essays that were later found on her computer sure seem to provide such evidence. The last stanza of this poem has provided the driving force behind Forever Family Foundation. If it was her wish (and a wish shared by a great many others) to communicate what the next realm was like, we owe it to our loved ones in the non-physical realm to do everything in our power to assist by receiving and facilitating spirit communication

The Phone Call

Shortly after Bailey's passing, I sought out traditional grief therapy, hoping that I could be prescribed some sort of mind-numbing medication that could make my reality disappear and the world go away. I started seeing a nurse practitioner grief therapist who chose to treat me via conversation rather the medication, much to my dismay. I suppose that I was making a small amount of progress in our sessions, but my grief was still overwhelming and suffocating.

As previously mentioned, we published Bailey's writings in a small book. After we received the first copies of the book, I decided to bring one along on my next appointment to present to my therapist. Due to a glitch in scheduling, when I arrived at the appointed time her office door was locked and unoccupied. I slipped a copy of the book under her door as a reminder that I had been there for our session. The therapist called the next day to explain the mix-up but left a message on my answering machine that sounded a bit unusual. She sounded a bit rattled, and simply said that she had an experience that she must share with me as soon as possible.

As it turned out, when she arrived at her office the next day for what she thought was our scheduled session, she immediately saw the book. Now having an hour block in her schedule without a patient, she sat down in her office to begin reading the book. She explained that while reading the book the lights in her office kept going on and off, despite it being a clear and sunny day with no other power disruptions in her office building. Since this had never happened before during the years that she occupied the same office, she found it a bit strange but certainly not an earth-shattering occurrence. As she continued reading, she came upon a story where Bailey, even though she was three years away from graduation, decided to write a graduation speech that she thought would one day deliver. In this speech she mentioned me as her personal hero. As soon as the therapist read this passage, as if on cue, her office telephone rang. She picked up the receiver, said hello, and heard the voice of a young girl giggling. The therapist continued to ask who was speaking, but simply heard the same continuous giggling until it faded away.

I do not know if the therapist had ever entertained the notion of an afterlife, but she told me that she "knew" that my daughter arranged this opportunity to get a message through to her dad. Could she have said this to me simply as a therapeutic tool to help me in my grief? Certainly yes, but based upon the conviction in her voice as she related the events to me, combined with the somewhat unsettling demeanor that she exhibited, I chose to believe what I was told and was grateful for the communication. Most of all it gave me a slight bit of comfort, a great deal of hope, and opened the door to a journey of exploration that continues today.

The Christmas Visit

The Christmas Eve following Bailey's death was not something that we had any desire to celebrate, even though we had a twenty-year tradition of spending it with our good friends. Kori came home from college and while sleeping had a dream visit from her sister Bailey, a visit that shook her to the core. She decided to get out of her bed and spend the night on the floor in our bedroom. During the early morning hours Phran felt something plop on our mattress, and looked over to see what she believed to be Kori sleeping on our bed. In the morning we learned that Kori never moved off the floor that night, and Phran instantly knew that she had a visit from Bailey.

We most often think of apparitions as having no physical form, and certainly no weight. Yet there are countless reports of people witnessing indentations and movement on beds and furniture, most often from unseen sources. However, in some cases as this one, visual recognition is made.

Escort to the Afterlife

Our family has spent Christmas Eve every year at the home of our good friends Joe and Linda. During these annual visits, my children got to spend the evening with Joe's mother and Linda's mother, who always joined us in the festivities. One November day Linda called her mom, Mackie, and sensed that something was wrong. Mackie was a breast cancer survivor who had done extremely well for the previous ten years, but something was very wrong on this day. Linda rushed over to Mackie's home which was a short five-minute drive. When she saw Mackie ailing, she called Mackie's physician, who told her to bring Mackie to the hospital, which was about an hour's drive away. By the time that they arrived at the hospital Mackie was in bad shape, conscious but somewhat incoherent. Acting on the doctor's instructions Mackie was admitted and sent to a patient room to wait for the doctor to arrive. Mackie was deteriorating fast and Linda was very concerned.

Linda was asked to wait outside the room as her mom was prepped. When Linda returned to the room, she was surprised to see her mom sitting up in bed and having a lively and coherent discussion with the nurse. She sat down to listen to the conversation and Mackie was telling the nurse about Bailey, my deceased daughter, and seemed surprised that the nurse could not see her. Shortly after this experience Mackie closed her eyes and passed early the next day, which happened to be Bailey's birthday.

*Deathbed visions are well known among a great many health professionals. When I heard about this occurrence from Linda I was not well versed in this phenomenon and tried to make sense of what happened. If this were simply a hallucination triggered by a dying brain, why would Mackie hallucinate about **my** daughter? Although Bailey liked her very much, they only saw each other once a year. Besides, Mackie had many personal losses in her own immediate family, including her husband. The only logical conclusion I could form was that Bailey was indeed there to assist Mackie in her crossing over. After examining this personal experience and learning about the historical anecdotal and scientific evidence about deathbed visions, I am now convinced that we **all** have assistance when we transition to the nonphysical realm.*

Timing Our Exit?

My mother was diagnosed with lung cancer and given a grim prognosis with a short time left to live. However, helped by a strict organic diet and natural supplements known to retard cancer growth, she did remarkably well for well over two years. However, about a month before her 90th birthday the disease caught up with her and she started to decline. Her appetite dwindled and her mental sharpness and clarity was replaced by occasional confusion as she seemed to slip in and out of consciousness. Knowing that the time was near, my brother joined Phran and me at my parents' home, as mom was in home hospice. It was the first time in recent years we were gathered in the same place at the same time. In the preceding couple of days, while she was still able to sit in a reclining chair, mom was talking to people that only she could see, including calling out to her mother. Others attributed this to hallucinations, but Phran and I knew exactly what was happening. At one point my father sat down in an empty chair that faced her recliner. My mother became very agitated and she insisted that he get up immediately and sit elsewhere. My father was probably insulted, but we later tried to explain her reason for asking him to move – he had sat on his mother-in-law.

When my mother could no longer move, was barely conscious and suffering from the pain, she spent the remaining time in her hospital bed. I leaned over and whispered that we were all there, we all loved her, and it was OK to let go. I reassured her that she would be seeing her parents, her sister, and her granddaughter soon. She opened her eyes and appeared to nod in acknowledgment. The next day, with us all standing by her bedside, I again whispered "OK mom, it's time to shed this broken body and fly – it's time to go home and meet everyone again." About an hour later she took flight.

The interesting postscript is that, at the same time, unbeknownst to me, my daughter and grandson were having a private prayer ceremony for "GiGima" in their home as they hoped for her to heal. After their prayers, my then four-year old grandson told my daughter "Mommy, I just looked out the window and saw GiGima flying on a rocket!" This was around the same time that GiGima, unbeknownst to them, had just passed.

Many believe that we often choose the exact time of our passing. This could be when certain family members are around, or perhaps the opposite. Sometimes the dying person needs some reassurance, as we are taught to "hold on" at all costs. There are also many accounts of the deceased person appearing before loved ones who are not aware of their passing. These cases are extremely evidential, don't you think?

My Personal Challenge

This book was written two years ago. It sat stored on my laptop, as I was simply too busy with foundation operations to pay further attention to its publication. In April of 2020, my wife Phran was diagnosed with pancreatic cancer. She was most likely harboring the disease for a long period before the diagnosis. I spent six months as her caregiver and watched helplessly as this force of nature, my light for the past forty-six years, suffered with this beast of an illness.

During her illness we never discussed her physical death as she was insistent on trying to maintain a positive frame of mind that would be conducive to healing. Near the end, when she came to the realization that all the healing protocols were not working, we managed to discuss a few details. This was difficult, as her body and brain were already ravaged as she survived each day in home hospice. One thing that she managed to communicate was that I needed to finish up and publish this book. Of course, I needed to honor this request.

As I write this it has been only two months since her passing, and my grief is suffocating, the same as it was for my daughter eighteen years ago. Phran and I were joined at the hip, were rarely apart, and I never imagined life without her. You may be wondering why I am mentioning this considering the subject matter of this book. After all, Phran and I have spent the last seventeen years educating the public about evidence of an afterlife and supporting the bereaved. This might lead you to believe that I am well prepared to handle the death of a loved one.

The simple truth is that we all grieve because we love. The more we love, the greater the pain of physical separation. But here is the thing. I know that I will survive this because I know that she still exists, and I know that I will see her again. Eventually light will begin to gradually dissipate the darkness. It will not happen overnight. Inner knowing that there is life after death is not a magic pill to alleviate grief, as the pain of not having them in the physical is profound. However, those who possess this knowing will emerge from the abyss and have a profound advantage over those who believe that death is final. Remember, mediums can do what they do because they tap into memories and personalities. If memories survive, so do those who physically die. It is as simple as that. And, if they survive, our fears of our loved ones being extinguished are unfounded.

CONCLUSION

I often refer to mediumship as a double-edged sword. At their best mediums can provide lifelines to those sinking in the abyss of sorrow and pain. At their worst they can propel the bereaved into deep chasms of despair. Some mediums deeply respect the work and are very much aware of the burden of responsibility inherent to the profession. Others look at the work simply as another way to make a living and lack the compassion and understanding so vital to the process.

To this day I find it very difficult to remain in the room when Forever Family Foundation hosts an event with a medium. You might ask why, as we have already certified the proficiency of the medium in spirit communication. The reason for my apprehension and anxiety is that I know that mediumship does not guarantee evidential connections to the spirit world, no matter how good the medium may be. I also can feel the tangible grief and sorrow among many of the attendees sitting in the audience, as they desperately need contact with their loved ones. I imagine the crowd as standing tenuously at a precipice, and the slightest wind in either direction can mean the difference between emotional healing and collapse. Those receiving strong evidential communications from their loved ones will most likely leave fortified by the knowledge that they still survive. However, for those who were not too sure to begin with and receive a poor non-evidential reading, they may leave convinced that death is final. So, instead of fulfilling the foundation's mission of educating the public about evidence suggesting life after death, the opposite notion may be conveyed. Of course, in a group setting, those not receiving a connection might take some solace in seeing others around them get evidential readings. After all, if someone else received evidence that their deceased loved one survived, it would be logical for everyone in the room to assume that their loved one survived as well.

Fortunately, the certified mediums have proven to be consistently evidential. That does not mean that they never have bad days and always connect with every sitter. It does mean that their connections are frequent, their evidence is strong, and the hits vastly outweigh the misses. It also means that most people who receive readings exhibit positive effects on their grief. I know that there are large numbers of such mediums in the world, and I hope that they can one day have their work recognized by credible organizations that evaluate the evidence objectively under controlled conditions.

The unfortunate fact is that for every one of the excellent mediums there are eight or nine that should not even be calling themselves mediums, let alone collecting money from the bereaved. These people face no repercussions, feel no responsibility, and keep inflicting emotional pain. What are we to do about this situation? The first step is to educate the public about the process itself, as I have attempted to do in this book. I would also like to see some sort of regulatory body that can oversee the profession by setting proficiency and ethical standards, as well as monitoring fraud. I know that we are not dealing with clear cut rules and practices in this arena, as the mediumship process itself is spontaneous in nature and difficult to evaluate. However, I am confident that such a board could be effective in reducing the fraud and identifying the capable practitioners. I know of no other profession, especially among those dealing with the emotional health of the public, that is not subject to scrutiny by an overseeing body.

Secondly, all mediums should be required to attend educational sessions with mental health professionals to learn about the grief process and ethics. There are too many practitioners that lack the compassion and understanding to sit before the bereaved. Understanding grief does not have anything to do with the process of receiving evidence, but it does give insight to the medium in the way the evidence should be presented to the sitter. I have witnessed some very evidential mediums convey information in such a callous and unfeeling manner that the sitter becomes deeply hurt, despite the accuracy of the communications. I understand that there is a fine line here, as I have previously described the role of the medium is to simply provide the evidence. However, for example, if the discarnate conveys the message to the medium that the sitter has a terminal disease, a condition unknown to the sitter, I think you would agree that there are preferred ways of letting the sitter know. The medium might suggest to the sitter that he/she visit their physician to get things checked out, as opposed to telling the sitter that mom says you have cancer and are going to die soon. I have witnessed the latter method, and the information turned out to be wrong! No matter how sure the medium is about the information they are receiving, a medium that fails to realize the possibility that they could be wrong is a train wreck waiting to happen.

It is also important to not look upon mediums as prophets or oracles sent from a divine source. Although some have been born with enhanced intuitive abilities, they are the same as the rest of us who exhibit a vast array of innate and learned skills. We need to create social, cultural, spiritual, and educational environments where phenomena that do not fit in with established physical laws can not only be openly discussed but encouraged. Every day, millions of people around the globe are privy to information and communication that defy mainstream thought. Some are oblivious to the reception due to their frames of reference. Others recognize the non-local information but are reluctant to share the experiences with others for fear of being judged or ridiculed. This fear is understandable, as it is frightening for one to accept that the world is different from what they have been taught. It is also unsettling to scientists, researchers, and educators whose foundations would crumble if non-physical phenomena turned out to be true.

So, the most important thing that we can all do is to start to **SHARE** what we know with family, friends, and acquaintances.

Share your telepathic experiences, your dream visits, precognitive moments, after death communications and signs, communications through mediums, and what you have learned about reincarnation, near death experiences and deathbed visions. The more we share, the more acceptable it becomes, and the closer we come to changing worldview about death. One day, as difficult as it may be to imagine now, we may look upon death as progression, the granting of freedom from physical shackles as we are birthed to a realm of unlimited potential.

Lastly, I would love to see the day when mediums are put out of business due to the widespread ability of us all to communicate directly with those who reside in other realms. I don't say this as a knock on the mediumship profession, but mediums would be the first to tell you that they believe that this ability is inherent to us all, was once the way it was before our intuitiveness became dormant, and will return as our consciousness evolves. Until then, we should all strive to see the spaces between the dots and remain open to the possibility that we all dance in a fluid sea of collective consciousness, a sea where it matters little if we have a physical body.

GLOSSARY OF TERMS

After death communication – broad term that encompasses varying ways in which the deceased contact those still in the physical realm

Afterlife – the term generally used to describe existence after physical death. The term could be considered a poor description if life is a continuum of growth and discovery.

Anecdotal – based upon personal accounts and experiences as opposed to laboratory research

Apport – the sudden appearance of a material object that is thought to be produced by non-physical means, usually by someone in the spirit realm

Akashic Field – the theory that all human events and thoughts ever to have occurred are stored in records or data fields. This includes the past, present and future.

Altered State – a broad term that encompasses changes in one's mental state that result in changes to subjective experiences.

Consciousness – normally thought of as the state of being aware, but to this date nobody has been able to determine the mechanism that allows this awareness. Many firmly believe that the brain produces consciousness, but others are convinced that our minds can act independently of the physical brain and survive physical death.

Deathbed vision – people approaching death report being visited by loved ones already deceased

Discarnate – not having a body. Usually used to describe a person in spirit

Ectoplasm – a viscous substance that is exuded from orifices in a medium's body. The substance is said to derive from discarnate entities and have spiritual energy.

Electronic Voice Phenomena – discarnate entities leaving voice messages on recording devices

Ghosts – manifestations by people in the spirit realm making themselves perceptible to those in the physical realm. People report seeing, hearing, feeling, and smelling ghosts, which appear to be conscious and interactive

Materialism – the theory that reality is governed and explained by physical matter, and all phenomena and consciousness are explainable by physical processes. Materialist science tends to discount all experiences that cannot be explained by known physical laws.

Mediumship – general term used to describe the process of mediums communicating with discarnate entities

Mediumshit – bad mediumship or mediums behaving badly

Near-death experience – people that are clinically dead or near-death report experiences of existence in other realms

Non-local consciousness – used to describe the theory that mind is not the same as brain, and that consciousness extends beyond the human body through non-physical means

Psychokinesis – used to describe the ability of the mind to affect matter

Psychometry – The process of touching an object that was held by another living or discarnate source to facilitate a connection to that entity.

Psi – a broad term that refers to psychic experiences that cannot be explained by known physical or biological mechanisms.

Psychic – referring to extrasensory perception, such as telepathy and other phenomena that do not involve the senses that many consider to be "normal."

Remote viewing – the process by which people can view distant targets using non-physical means

Reincarnation – the concept that after death one's soul or consciousness returns to the physical in another body.

Séance – a small gathering of people that sit together for the purpose of communicating with spirit. The term is usually associated with physical and trance mediums who utilize the collective energy of the group as they connect with spirit

Sitter – regarding mediumship, the person who is receiving the reading from a medium

Spirit – in the context of mediumship, referring to the entity no longer in the physical realm (the deceased}.

Spirit communication – exchange of information between entities living in the physical realm and those in an afterlife realm

Spirit Guides – entities in the afterlife who were once embodied and now assist mediums and others in the physical world.

Super Psi Hypothesis – similar concept to the Akashic Records in that the mind exists in an information field that can be accessed. Some use this hypothesis to argue against survival of consciousness, claiming that we are simply retrieving information as opposed to communicating with the dead

Survival of consciousness – the hypothesis that our minds, or consciousness, continue after physical death

Synchronicity – when seemingly separate and non-related events come together in a meaningful and purposeful way.

Telepathy – communication that is mind to mind without the use of physical means

Wannamedium – a person who desires to become a medium, sometimes for the wrong reasons

Recommended Reading

Afterlife Encounters: Ordinary People, Extraordinary Experiences –
Dianne Arcangel, MS
The Gift: The Extraordinary Experiences of Ordinary People –
Sally Rhine Feather, PhD & Michael Schmicker
Opening Heaven's Door: Investigating Stories of Life, Death, and
What Comes After – Patricia Pearson
41 Signs of Hope – Dave Kane
Telephone Calls from the Dead – Callum Cooper, PhD
The Afterlife is Real – Theresa Cheung
Changed in a Flash: One Woman's Near-Death Experience and
Why a Scholar Thinks It Empowers Us All – Elizabeth G Krohn
and Jeffrey Kripal, PhD
There Is No Death and There Are No Dead – Tom & Lisa Butler
The Departed Among the Living: An Investigative Study of Afterlife
Encounters – Erlendur Haraldsson, PhD
The ESP Enigma: The Scientific Case for Psychic Phenomena –
Dianne Hennacy Powell, MD
Entangled Minds: Extrasensory Experiences in a Quantum Reality –
Dean Radin, PhD
Limitless Mind: A Guide to Remote Viewing and Transformation of
Consciousness – Russell Targ
Raising Intuitive Children: Guide Your Children to Know and Trust
Their Gifts – Carol B Goode , PhD
Real Magic: Ancient Wisdom, Modern Science, and a Guide to the
Secret Power of the Universe – Dean Radin, PhD
Psychic Intuition: Everything You Ever Wanted to Ask but Were
Afraid to Know – Nancy Du Tertre

Proof Positive: Metaphysical Wisdom – Doreen Molloy

Consulting Spirit: A Doctor's Experience with Practical Mediumship – Ian Rubenstein, MD

Spirits … They Are Present – Janet Mayer

Where Two Worlds Meet – Janet Nohavec

The Light Between Us: Stories from Heaven – Lessons for the Living – Laura Lynne Jackson

Mind Beyond Brain: Buddhism, Science, and the Paranormal – David E. Presti PhD

Talking to the Dead: Kate and Maggie Fox and the Rise of Spiritualism – Barbara Weisberg

Return to Life: Extraordinary Cases of Children Who Remember Past Lives – Jim Tucker, MD

Reincarnation, Channeling and Possession: A Parapsychologist's Handbook – Loyd Auerbach, MS

I Saw A Light and Came Here: Children's Experiences of Reincarnation – Erlendur Haraldsson Phd & James Matlock PhD

The End of Materialism: How Evidence of the Paranormal Is Bringing Science and Spirit Together – Charles Tart PhD

The Gold Leaf Lady and Other Parapsychological Investigations – Stephen Braude, PhD

The Man Who Could Fly: St. Joseph of Copertino and the Mystery of Levitation – Michael Grosso PhD

The Flip: Epiphanies of Mind and the Future of Knowledge – Jeffrey J. Kripal PhD

The PK Man: A True Story of Mind Over Matter – Jeffrey Mishlove, PhD

The Purpose-Guided Universe: Believing in Einstein, Darwin, and God – Bernard Haisch, PhD

Science of the Soul, The Afterlife, and The Shift – Claude Swanson, PhD

Unbelievable: Investigations into Ghosts, Poltergeists, Telepathy, and Other Unseen Phenomena, from the Duke Parapsychology Laboratory – Stacy Horn

Irreducible Mind: Toward a Psychology for the 21st Century –
Edward Kelly PhD & Emily Kelly PhD

Science and the Afterlife Experience: Evidence for the Immortality
of Consciousness – Chris Carter

21 Days into the Afterlife: A scientific and literary journey that may
change your life – Piero Calvi-Parisetti MD

The Force Is with Us: The Higher Consciousness That Science
Refuses to Accept – Thomas Walker D.C.

Surviving Death: A Journalist Investigates Evidence for an Afterlife –
Leslie Kean

Unseen Forces: The Integration of Science, Reality and You –
Robert Davis, PhD

A Paranormal Casebook: Ghost Hunting in the New Millennium –
Loyd Auerbach, MS

Conversations with Ghosts – Alex Tanous

Esp, Hauntings and Poltergeists: A Parapsychologist's Handbook –
Loyd Auerbach, MS

The Miracle of Death – Betty Kovacs, PhD

Testimony of Light: An Extraordinary Message of Life After Death –
Helen Greaves

A Lawyer Presents the Evidence for the Afterlife – Victor & Wendy
Zammit

Immortal Remains: The Evidence for Life After Death – Stephen
Braude, PhD

Is There an Afterlife?: A Comprehensive Overview of the Evidence –
David Fontana, PhD

The Afterlife Revealed: What Happens After We Die – Michael
Tymn

The Afterlife Unveiled: What the Dead are Telling Us About Their
World – Stafford Betty, PhD

The Last Frontier: Exploring the Afterlife and Transforming Our
Fear of Death – Julia Assante, PhD

The Risen: Dialogues of Love, Grief & Survival – August Goforth

The Unobstructed Universe – Stewart Edward White

The Blue Island: and Other Spiritualist Writings (Life on Other Worlds Series) – W.T Stead

Induced After-Death Communication: A New Therapy for Healing Grief and Trauma – Allan Botkin, PhD

Messages & Miracles: Extraordinary Experiences of the Bereaved – Louis LaGrand, PhD

Life After Loss: Conquering Grief and Finding Hope – Raymond Moody, MD & Dianne Arcangel, MS

On Death and Dying – Elizabeth Kubler-Ross, MD

Love Knows No Death: A Guided Workbook for Grief Transformation – Piero Calvi-Parisetti, MD

Life at Death – Kenneth Ring, PhD

A Glimpse of Heaven: The Remarkable World of Spiritually Transformative Experiences – Carla Wills-Brandon, PhD

Proof of Heaven: A Neurosurgeon's Journey into the Afterlife – Eben Alexander III, MD

The Big Book of Near-Death Experiences: The Ultimate Guide to What Happens When We Die – PMH Atwater LhD

The End of Death: How Near-Death Experiences Prove the Afterlife – Admir Serrano

When Did You Ever Become Less by Dying? Afterlife: The Evidence – Stafford Betty PhD

The Handbook of Near-Death Experiences: Thirty Years of Investigation – Janice Miner Holden PhD

Suicide: What Really Happens in the Afterlife? – Pamela Rae Heath, MD & Jon Klimo, PhD

Dreamscaping: New Techniques for Understanding Yourself and Others – Stanley Krippner, PhD

The Three "Only" Things: Tapping the Power of Dreams, Coincidence, and Imagination – Robert Moss

Exploring the World of Lucid Dreaming – Stephen LaBerge

Journeys Out of the Body – Robert Monroe

Adventures Beyond the Body: How to Experience Out-of-Body Travel – William Buhlman

Channeling: Investigations on Receiving Information from Paranormal Sources, Second Edition – Jon Klimo, PhD

"Opening to Channel, How to Connect with Your Guide " – Sanaya Roman & Duane Packer

Mind Science: Meditation Training for Practical People – Charles Tart, PhD

The Beginner's Guide to Meditation (Beginners Ser.) – Shinzen Young

UFOs: Generals, Pilots, and Government Officials Go on the Record – Leslie Kean

The Energy Cure: Unraveling the Mystery of Hands-On Healing – William Bengston, PhD

The Gift of Shamanism: Visionary Power, Ayahuasca Dreams, and Journeys to Other Realms – Itzhak Beery

Merchants of Light – The Consciousness That Is Changing the World – Betty Kovacs, PhD

Made in the USA
Las Vegas, NV
17 January 2021